HIGH FLIERS

Airmen of Achievement in Wartime

PHILIP KAPLAN

Skyhorse Publishing

Skyhorse Publishing books may be purchased in bulk at special discounts for sales promotion, corporate gifts, fund-raising, or educational purposes. Special editions can also be created to specifications. For details, contact the Special Sales Department, Skyhorse Publishing, 307 West 36th Street, 11th Floor, New York, NY 10018 or info@skyhorsepublishing.com.

Skyhorse® and Skyhorse Publishing® are registered trademarks of Skyhorse Publishing, Inc.®, a Delaware corporation.

Visit our website at www.skyhorsepublishing.com.

10 9 8 7 6 5 4 3 2 1

Library of Congress Cataloging-in-Publication Data is available on file.

Cover design by Rain Saukas
Cover photo credit: Jack Ilfrey

Print ISBN: 978-1-5107-0513-5
Ebook ISBN: 978-1-5107-0518-0

Printed in the United States of America

CONTENTS

Group Captain Brian Kingcome.
Ninety-two Squadron, Royal
Air Force.

BRIAN KINGCOME

On one relatively quiet day late in the Battle of Britain, Ninety-two Squadron was finally scrambled in the mid-morning with Brian Kingcome in the lead. Vectored to intercept enemy raiders over Maidstone in Kent, the British pilots located the German formation, broke it up, and sent them packing for their French base. It had been a typical operation for Brian, a brief, successful encounter. With his ammunition used up, he headed back towards Biggin Hill, having found himself in that strange yet familiar empty-sky phenomenon, except for three Spitfires in the far distance, seconds after the air fight. Now it was midday and the weather was glorious; the sky cloudless. He had missed breakfast and was hungry. "I put my nose down to head straight for home and lunch, but then thought I might as well kill two birds with one brick and decided to throttle back and practice a 'dead stick' forced landing; one with simulated engine failure.

"It was breathtakingly stupid behaviour. The skies of Kent were at all times a hostile environment, whatever the illusion of emptiness, yet here was I, as operationally experienced as anyone, casually putting at risk my aircraft and my life—a vital, valuable piece of equipment and a trained pilot, each disproportionately crucial, with supplies of both dwindling fast. I can only put the action down to an overconfidence fostered by constant exposure to the dawn-to-dusk rotation of 'take off, climb, engage, land, refuel, rearm, take off, climb, engage . . .' two, three or sometimes four times a day, familiarity reducing what had begun as exciting, adrenaline-pumping action to mere routine. I had grown blasé. Perhaps I needed to be shot up to reawaken me to reality.

"And here I was, oblivious to danger, admiring the view, enjoying the sensation of speed as I pushed the nose down towards distant Biggin Hill, forgetting the fighter pilot's golden rule to watch his tail however safe he thought he might be—always to watch his tail. I was sailing in a dream when my reveries were rudely shattered by an almighty thump to the back of the right leg. It came as a bit of a shock to one who believed himself alone with 20,000 clear feet between himself and other human company. Worse was to follow: a rattling clatter as if someone were violently shaking a giant bucket full of pebbles close to my ear. Still it took me a further moment or two to realize that this sound was the jarring impact of bullets striking in and around my cockpit. Glancing down at my leg, I saw blood welling out of the top of my flying boot, and knew that what had felt like a thump from a blunt instrument had also been a bullet. I felt no pain. With bullet wounds the pain comes later.

"I jerked myself around, but could see no sign of anything except the three Spitfires I had noticed before. Now they drew alongside, peered at me briefly, then peeled away. Whether they had mistaken me for a German, or whether they were white knights who had shot someone else off my tail, was something I was never to know. I was left with blood flowing out of the top of my flying-boot and my ailerons gone suddenly sluggish.

"Here was just the sort of situation I had often mentally rehearsed, behaving with dignity, competence, and calm, emulating those phlegmatic First World War movie heroes of *The Dawn Patrol* and *Hell's Angels* sitting imperturbably in smoke-filled cockpits, nonchalantly saluting their opponents as, engulfed in flames, they began a long spiral to a fiery death. I regret to say I failed dismally to match the image of the Errol Flynn prototype. I was panic-stricken, gripped in a blind, paralyzing terror. This could not be happening to me. This only happened to the other Chap! For what felt like a century, though it could only have been a few moments, I sat rigid and disbelieving, my stomach churning. Here was the real thing. This was what it felt like. All at once I had become the other chap for whom I had always felt sorry, though I had never lost any sleep about it.

"The effect was devastating: one minute relaxed and carefree, in total control with nothing more dramatic in mind than a simulated forced landing and the day's lunch menu; the next, inhabiting a doomed aircraft at 20,000 feet, losing blood at a rate that suggested consciousness might slip away at any moment with death following within minutes. Death: so far I had managed to keep him discreetly imprisoned in the back of my mind, vague and ill-defined, a subject fit for black humour, not to be taken too seriously. Now he became a terrifying reality so close I could smell him. Or was this simply the smell of my own fear, unlocking feelings I thought I had defused and put safely aside?"

Then the panic was gone; Brian was calm, his thoughts rational. The fear, however, was still present, but now it was working for him. His adrenaline was pumping and his brain working efficiently again. He quickly evaluated the situation and realized he had two options: either stay with the airplane in the hope that he could bring it back to Biggin without the control cables parting at the last minute when he was too low to jump, or simply bail out to, hopefully, save himself. The success of this latter choice depended on his opening his parachute before passing

Group Captain Brian Kingcome in his Spitfire cockpit, and members of No Ninety-two Squadron at RAF Biggin Hill in 1940.

out from loss of blood, and then not bleeding to death on the way down. His imagination kicked in at that point with visions of jumping into freezing, hostile space . . . but, all things considered, bailing out seemed to him his best option. Still, the Spitfire was not on fire and was reasonably stable and he still felt secure in the cockpit. It was only the blood loss that motivated him to leave that formerly cozy environment.

Now he had to quickly assess the possible ways of bailing out. Going over the side was probably not the best choice due to the risk of being blown back onto the tailplane and maybe cut in half, which had been the fate of at least one fighter pilot. A better way, supposedly, was to roll the airplane on its back, jettison the canopy, undo the straps and leads, and allow gravity to take over. But with aileron problems, Brian was not keen to trust the rolling maneuver. He decided instead to dump the canopy, undo the straps etc., and shove the control column hard forward, which he hoped would catapult him out of the cockpit. He got as far as undoing his straps when he was sucked from the airplane and thrust like a rag doll into space, tumbling uncontrollably. The forces acting on him were brutal and literally bruising. He later estimated that he had left the Spitfire at between 350 and 400 mph, but soon slowed to the terminal velocity of the human body falling through space, about 120 mph. He felt relaxed, and the lack of oxygen and his blood loss were shielding him from fear. There was no sense of falling or wind. In a semiconscious state he plunged earthward, with no real sense of how long he had been free-falling or how far he had fallen. He was somehow reminded that he had lost a lot of blood and had to get down fast. Then he recalled that the flight had climbed through a layer of cumulus cloud at about 4,000 feet and thus knew that he could fall about 15,000 feet before he had to open his parachute. He seemed to recall too, that his own parachute had been away for routine inspection that morning and he had grabbed the nearest available one as he left for the dispersal. One of the parachute packers had warned him that that one too was due for inspection and he ought to take another one, but he couldn't be bothered, believing, as most pilots seemed to do, that they were invulnerable.

The moment came to open the 'chute and when he pulled the rip cord it worked just as it had been designed to do. "There was only a split second in which to wonder whether I had made a bad choice of parachute before, with a satisfying crack, it snapped open and braked my downward rush with a bone-cracking jerk" and he began slowly descending towards the lush patchwork countryside of Kent. His senses cleared somewhat and he noticed that he had instinctively pulled the rip cord just hard enough to release the canopy while retaining the cord itself. The natural reaction when bailing out was to pull the rip cord as hard as one could and then toss it away as it came off in your hand. It had been drummed into him though, to keep the thing or be charged ten shillings, nearly a day's pay, if you failed to bring it back. Ten shillings was the equivalent of a night out in London or four nights in the local pubs. He had been well trained. He recalled the descent as he approached the ground from several hundred feet above it. "I dangled in the harness, swaying gently, studying the ground beneath me. What astonished me was not what I could see—I was used to that—but what I could

hear: the sounds that rose up to me from the ground. I was accustomed to a noisy cockpit and earphones that cut out all other sound, but now, as I drifted down the last thousand feet or so, the silence was broken by car horns, by cattle lowing, even by human voices, which came up to me with startling clarity. As I floated down over open farmland I could see below me a small group of agricultural workers armed with pitchforks and other businesslike farm implements heading across to the field towards which I was drifting. For the first time since parting company with my aircraft I began to feel a definite alarm. There had been stories of parachuting Allied airmen being beaten up and, on one occasion, even killed by incensed locals, working on the patriotic assumption that if they had been shot down then they must be the enemy. To complicate matters, I was wearing a German Mae West [that] I had commandeered from the body of the crew member of the Ju 88 [that I had shot down previously]. Apprehensively I gazed down at the group who gazed up at me, gripping the formidable tools of their trade."

Brian landed hard, permanently damaging a disc in his back and knocking the breath out of him, but he managed to sit up quickly and pull the German life-jacket off to show the farm workers his RAF uniform. Fortunately, they smiled and seemed friendly, having seen his Spitfire crash nearby. One of them offered, "We'd better get you to a hospital before you bleed to death" staring at Brian's blood-soaked trouser leg. Once again he was to suffer excessively and needlessly at the hands of a less than competent surgeon who, in probing along the track of the bullet wound, cut through a blood vessel. The act caused the two ends of the vessel

to spring apart, whereupon he lost them. He then complicated the situation further by cutting down the leg in search of the missing items. Failing to locate them he elected to simply stuff the wound with dressing, sew it up and cover the leg in plaster. When Brian regained consciousness and learned from a concerned nurse what had been done to him, he got word to the station adjutant at Biggin Hill and got himself transferred to a hospital near the base where a more skilful surgeon located the bullet by x-ray and removed it through a small incision. After a six-week recovery Kingcome was back with his squadron.

While Brian waited to become fit enough to be operational again, Ninety-two Squadron received a new commander, Johnny Kent, a well-known and accomplished Canadian who had recently commanded one of the Polish fighter squadrons. Early in spring 1941, the squadron was detached to RAF Manston on the Kentish coast to protect that hot little corner of England.

The pilots of RAF Fighter Command had gone on the offensive and were flying regular sweep attacks on targets in German-occupied France. The British fighter force was growing in strength while the Luftwaffe was weaker in the west, having had to transfer many units to the Soviet front, leaving the Channel front with less German protection. Looking to capitalize on an opportunity to gain air supremacy in the Channel area, the Royal Air Force was poised to take advantage of any such openings.

Since June 1941, the two powerful and modern German pocket battleships, *Scharnhorst* and *Gneisenau*, and the battle cruiser *Prinz Eugen*, had been

The remains of a painted RAF eagle on a wall at Fowlmere near Cambridge.

sheltering in the French port of Brest. They had been bottled up there and under frequent attack by RAF Bomber Command aircraft, while the harbor was blockaded by continuous Royal Navy submarine patrols. The British were protecting their convoy traffic in the Channel from attack by these German warships and, though the bombing raids on the warships were largely ineffectual, they did serve to keep the threat of these menacing enemy vessels contained for the time being.

Concerned that the Allies were planning to open a new war front in Scandinavia, Hitler ordered that the three German warships be moved from Brest to Norway via Germany. If they were routed around Scotland, they faced the possibility of a battle with units of the British Home Fleet, then stationed at Scapa Flow, in the Orkneys. If, on the other hand, they were sent through the English Channel, they would be exposed to

the attentions of the RAF, to British warships and coastal gun batteries. They chose the latter option, believing that, with the support and protection of the Luftwaffe fighter force, their battleships and battle cruiser could make a successful "Channel Dash," which they called Operation Thunderbolt.

It was Group Captain Victor Beamish, then commander of RAF Kenley, west of Biggin Hill, who, on February 12, 1942, was flying an impromptu sweep into France with another Kenley Spitfire pilot, when he happened to spot and report a little flotilla of E-boats and destroyers escorting the three German warships off the coast near Le Touquet.

Robert Stanford Tuck, then wing commander at Biggin Hill, had asked Brian Kingcome to take command of Seventy-Two Squadron which, at that point, was on temporary detachment at Gravesend, one of Biggin's satellite

airfields, where the squadron that day was on "thirty minutes" availability status. Ensconced in their quarters at Cobham Hall, home of the Earl of Darnley, the officers of the Seventy-Two read newspapers and tried to catch up on some sleep that morning, until noon when the telephone rang bringing them to readiness. Moments later they were at the dispersal and ordered to "cockpit standby."

Confusion reigned throughout Fighter Command over the next half hour as to what was actually happening in the Channel. Over that period, Kingcome was given four different sets of instructions before finally being ordered to take off immediately and head for Manston at full throttle, where he would meet four more Spitfire squadrons in the air over the base. The other squadrons would form up behind Seventy-Two Squadron, all of which Kingcome would command. When they

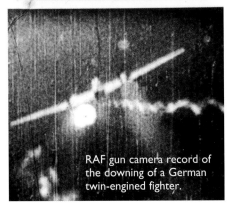

RAF gun camera record of the downing of a German twin-engined fighter.

rendezvoused, six Fleet Air Arm Swordfish torpedo bombers would be scrambled from Manston, to be escorted by the wing of Spitfires to the Straits of Dover where some enemy naval activity was evidently under way. Several British motor-torpedo boats were known to be engaging a German E-boat flotilla there. Kingcome considered all of this on the way to Manston and thought about the Fairey Swordfish biplane, which, in his view, was "a testimony to the navy's attachment to the pre-historic: antediluvian airplanes with fixed undercarriages and three crew members crammed into two open cockpits. They had been designed to function as torpedo carriers and this was a task they could just about manage, though the weight of a tor-pedo left them with a top speed of between 85 and 90 knots—about or below the stalling speed for most other aircraft of their generation."

He knew too, that there was no shortage of guts, heroism, and dedica-tion among the crews of the Fleet Air Arm and that, to some extent at least, counterbalanced the obvious deficien-cies of their aircraft. This was shown in a naval action of May 1940 when the great German battleship *Bismarck*, easily superior in most respects to the capital ships of the Royal Navy, out-ran and outshot the British warships that were trying to sink her. It took a torpedo attack by the obsolescent Swordfish from the carrier HMS *Ark Royal*, with an admittedly lucky strike when one of the weapons hit *Bismarck* in her rudder, seriously dam-aging her steering gear, to pave the way for the British warships *Rodney, Dorsetshire,* and *King George V* to final-ly send her to the bottom.

As Kingcome, in the lead of nine other Spitfires, arrived over Manston, he was surprised to find the six

Swordfish biplanes already airborne and orbiting the airfield. He was more surprised to discover that none of the other Spitfire squadrons scheduled for the operation had appeared. As soon as they spotted the Spitfires, the Swordfish pilots straightened and headed off without waiting for any more Spitfires to show up. Brian was surprised yet again when the Swordfish flight set course due east rather than south towards Dover, as he had expected. The torpedo bombers were heading out over the North Sea at wave-top height; the sea was rough and immediately overhead lay thick, intermittent cloud cover, which made the visibility only 200 yards at best. As the top speed of the Swordfish was only equal to the stall-ing speed of the Spitfire, the only way the small Spitfire force could maintain visual contact with the Swordfish, without spinning into the sea, was to weave behind the torpedo planes in large figure eights. Had the other Spitfire squadrons arrived as planned, the coordination of their movements might well have proven disastrous.

A few moments away from the English coast, the Spitfires were attacked by enemy fighters but the British pilots quickly repelled them without sustaining any casualties. Shortly after the encounter, Brian sighted "the most magisterial warship you could have imagined. Its sinister beauty and overpowering menace were palpable. Mentally I began to . . . congratulate the Royal Navy. At last, it seemed they had made a dramatic move up-market and got themselves a real ship of battle for the present and future." Then it seemed that every gun in the mighty warship opened up in Brian's direction. The Royal Navy did have a reputation among airmen for shooting first and asking questions afterwards. But the six Swordfish bore in on the great vessel without the slightest hesitation. Their intent was clear. The Spitfire pilots were uncertain; some thought they might be about to witness a torpedo attack on a capital ship of the British fleet.

At that point the big ship lowered her guns and began firing shells and salvos into the sea ahead of the approaching Swordfish. Huge towers of white spray erupted in front of the plodding torpedo planes which, somehow, were able to dodge the worst of the gunfire. Brian thought that one of the Swordfish had been hit, but he wasn't sure about it. The small troup of Swordfish never faltered. They drove on until reaching torpedo range. There was nothing the frustrated Spitfire pilots could do to help. And then Kingcome and the British fighter pilots were bounced by a swarm of Me 109s.

The fourth surprise of the day for Brian was the appearance of a new German fighter in the midst of the 109s; it was his first contact with the Focke-Wulf Fw 190, an impressive, radial-engined single-seater about which the pilots of the Seventy-Two had not yet been briefed. He later learned that the German commander in the air was General of the Fighter Arm Adolf Galland, probably the Luftwaffe's most celebrated fighter leader and one of its greatest fighter pilots.

Of the six Swordfish, none survived the attack. Of the eighteen Swordfish aircrew, five were later rescued from the water. After dealing with the audacious torpedo planes, the mighty battle cruiser *Prinz Eugen* rejoined the *Scharnhorst* and *Gneisenau* and the three of them, together with their protective flotilla, moved on to vanish in the North Sea gloom.

The Spitfires had been airborne for just over an hour when they landed back at Gravesend, some of them shot up from the encounter with the enemy

fighters. The operation had been an utter disaster for the British, whose intelligence facility had been entirely outfoxed by the enemy, as evidenced by the decision to employ the six Swordfish in a hopeless cause on a suicidal mission against three such formidable warships, wasting the lives of all but five of the air crewmen. The British military planners had been fooled too, after the RAF's last bombing attack on the German battleships in Brest harbor appeared to have damaged the vessels sufficiently for the British to call off their surveillance and blockade of the harbor. The Germans had pulled off a magnificent ruse by cosmetically dressing the decks of the warships with debris to make them look from the air as though they had suffered severe damage. British photo interpreters took the bait and the planners did just as the Germans thought they would. After clearing the decks, the enemy warships were able to steal out of Brest on their Channel Dash. Of the Swordfish crews, the navigation officer of *Scharnhorst* later stated, "Their bravery was devoted and incredible. They knowingly and ungrudgingly gave their all to their country and went to their doom without hesitation."

In the summer of 1942, Brian Kingcome was posted to Kenley to take over as Wing Commander Flying. His Command was known as the "Canadian Wing" and was made up of Nos. 401, 402, 412 and 416 Squadrons and, at last, he felt he had landed in a virtually perfect situation. The Station Commander at Kenley then was Group Captain Richard Atcherley, a man Brian liked and respected, and he had charge of four fine Spitfire squadrons.

The job of the Kenley Wing was twofold: fighter sweeps penetrating as far over France as they could go,

attempting to lure German fighters into combat; the other to provide fighter escort protection for the heavy bombers of the U.S. Army Air Force in their daylight bombing missions at a point in the war when the Americans could muster relatively few planes and crews to face a powerful Luftwaffe on the defensive. Due to the still quite limited range of the Spitfires available at the time, Kingcome's pilots could only shepherd the bombers during the first, and least vulnerable, portion of their missions, or rendezvous with them for that same part of the return trip. For the rest of the journey, the bomber crews were largely on their own, reliant on their own gunners and their clever "box" formations for protection through maximum cross fire.

At about this time, some RAF fighter squadrons were beginning to be equipped with a significantly improved Spitfire, the Mk IX. It featured a new Merlin engine, the 61, with a two-stage, two-speed supercharger which overcame one of the Spitfire's few weaknesses. Previously, the airplane simply began to run short of power as it climbed through about 15,000 feet and the thinning air robbed the earlier Merlin of energy. This engine produced a whole new power regime for higher altitudes as the new supercharger kicked in around the limits of the old engine, enabling the plane to operate efficiently at far higher altitudes. In August, Kingcome's 402 Squadron was the first in his wing to be equipped with the Mk IXs and, as Wing Commander, he immediately commandeered one for his personal aircraft and had it marked with his initials as part of the fuselage code. "The first time I flew the Mark IX I could hardly believe the experience. The effect was magical. I had expected an increase in power, but nothing to match the reality. To enhance the dramatic effect,

Group Captain Brian Kingcome, who commanded Ninety-two Squadron at Biggin Hill.

the second stage cut in automatically without warning. One minute I was, relaxed and peaceful, as I climbed at a leisurely pace towards 15,000 feet, anticipating a small surge of extra power as I hit the magic number. The next minute it was as though a giant hand had grabbed hold of me, cradled me in its palm—like a shot-putter his weight—and given me the most terrific shove forwards and upwards. The shock was so great that I almost baled [sic] out. It literally took my breath away. It was exhilarating, a feeling I could never forget. I yearned at once for a chance to demonstrate this astonishing new tool to the Germans."

Another organization then receiving the new Mk IX Spitfires was the American Eagle Squadron, actually composed of three squadrons (No 71 stationed at Debden, Essex, No 121 at North Weald, Essex and No 133 at Biggin Hill). The Eagles had been formed of American volunteer fliers in the days before the United States had entered the war. They were squadrons of RAF Fighter Command and their pilots wore the RAF uniform and flew its aircraft. After the Japanese attack on Pearl Harbor in December 1941, the United States declared war on Japan and Germany, and with the presence of the U.S. Army Air Force in Britain, the Eagles would soon transfer to the USAAF and become the Fourth Fighter Group, based at Debden, an outfit that would finish the war as the highest scoring American fighter group in the European Theatre of Operations. For most (but not all) of the Eagles, the transfer was not mandatory; they could if they wished remain with the RAF, and some did so despite the better pay of pilots in the USAAF. One of these was Carroll "Red" McColpin, the commander of 133 Squadron. "I knew that a big mission to Morlaix was coming up, but

I'd been ordered to transfer to the USAAF. Ordered. I kept delaying it week after week.

"We were down at Biggin Hill, but 133 was being moved up to Great Sampford, near Debden. The mission was being laid on . . . then off . . . then on again. I decided I wouldn't go and leave the outfit until the mission was over with. I was gonna lead that mission. Then General 'Monk' Hunter called up from Fighter Command Headquarters of the Eighth Air Force and said, 'I understand you haven't transferred,' and I said, 'Yes sir.' He just said, 'Well you get your butt in there and transfer, right now!' To which I came back, 'Sir, I'm waiting for this Morlaix mission and I'm trying to keep enough boys in here to run it 'cause it's a big one.' 'To heck with that . . . you get in there and transfer,' Hunter replied. 'Well, sir,' I said, 'You understand that I'm in the Royal Air Force, sir, and I have an ops instruction which says we are going to Morlaix when they lay it on. I'm the CO here, and I've got my squadron on the line.' With that he snorted and hung up. About an hour later I got a call from an air marshal in the group. 'McColpin, do you take orders from me?' I said, 'I certainly do, sir. Yes, sir.' That's how I came to transfer over."

When the Morlaix raid was finally laid on it was a disaster and a tragic way for the Eagles to bow out of the Royal Air Force.

British pilot Gordon Brettell was made commander of 133 and led the Morlaix mission in place of McColpin.

The mission called for the Eagles, along with other Fighter Command Spitfire squadrons, including Brian Kingcome's, to escort American bombers in an attack on a Brest peninsula target. They were to cross the widest part of the English Channel and fly over a heavily defended area.

At Great Sampford, 133 Squadron awaited transfer into the American Air Force, but they would still fly the Morlaix mission before the transfer came about. They, along with the other Spitfire squadrons, were sent down to Bolt Head, a blustery and desolate forward airfield on cliffs between Dartmouth and Plymouth, Devon. At Bolt Head they were to be refueled and briefed for the mission, and join up with the other squadrons. On the flight from Great Sampford down to Devon the weather was deteriorating and began to threaten the impending mission.

Crucially, without the leadership and discipline of Red McColpin that day, the pilots of 133 were overly nonchalant and cavalier. Most of them didn't even attend the briefing for the raid. Gordon Brettell and one other pilot were the only ones briefed. In the briefing, they were told, incorrectly, that there would be a thirty-five knot headwind at their cruising altitude of 28,000 feet. Incredibly, the exact take-off time of the bombers, and the time for their rendezvous with the fighters were unknown and not provided in the briefing. McColpin had a reputation among the Eagle commanders as a brilliant planner with exceptional attention to detail. Those qualities were blatantly missing on the day of the Morlaix raid. Even the takeoff of the fighter mass was chaotic, with a number of near-collisions; the pilots received incorrect instructions about radio frequencies and some neglected to bring their maps and escape kits.

Thirty-six Spitfires were airborne from Bolt Head, fitted with auxiliary fuel tanks and en route to meet the bombers. Kingcome: "We had been flying for hardly more than five or ten minutes before a layer of cloud began to gather below us. It was thick and mountainous and the sea was entirely

concealed by the time we were half-way across the Channel. For about twenty-five minutes we continued climbing steadily until we had reached to around 20,000 feet and were, by our calculations, directly above the French coast. We then went into a gentle orbit as we began to scan about us for the Flying Fortresses. The sky seemed empty, but then I spotted them a long way to the south, little more than dots on the horizon and evidently forced up by the towering clouds to about the same altitude as ours. I thought it odd that they were so far from the target area. Then, as we watched, they turned northeast and headed for home. The heavy cloud cover must have made them abort the raid. We then turned for home ourselves."

After flying due north for roughly a half hour, Brian and the other Spitfire pilots thought they must be nearing the English coast, but the massive cumulus clouds were stretching ahead and below, seemingly without a break. On the outbound flight the sky over England had been clear. They had been climbing slowly to 20,000 feet and now, they had been flying straight and level at that altitude and should certainly be at or inbound of the coast and the sky should have been clear. He knew that in the hour or so that they had been airborne, the weather could not possibly have changed that dramatically. The other thing that worried Brian was his inability to get a response from ground control each time he tried. He knew ground control would be listening for a call from him and was puzzled by their failure to respond.

Contrary to the Met officer's briefing prediction of a thirty-five knot headwind on the course of the fighters to Morlaix, both the bombers and the fighters had been shoved along by a 100-knot tailwind. Far ahead of the fighters, above the solid cloud cover, the bombers had unknowingly flown across the Bay of Biscay and continued on to the Pyrenees mountains where they realized their predicament and dumped their bombloads. They then turned for home and spotted their Spitfire escort. By that time, all of the bombers and fighters had ceased to register on English radar plots and any communications between their bases in England and the fighters and bombers was hopeless.

The Spitfires had been in the air for more than two hours and, convinced that they had to be near their bases, began to let down through a gap they found in the cloud cover . . . except for Kingcome and his squadron. "I was sorely pressed to follow, but . . . found myself hesitating. Perhaps I was being too clever by half. The time element, alongside the fact that the coast was south-facing, surely confirmed that this could be nowhere else than Devon. There could not be another south coast within a hundred miles. Nevertheless the inconsistent weather pattern and ground control's sphinx-like silence continued to feed my profound unease. I decided that 401 Squadron ought to press on."

The flying range of the Spitfires was between two and a quarter and two and a half hours. There was still no response from ground control. Moments later, the cloud began to thin, to Brian's intense relief. But when it cleared he found that the squadron was over an endless expanse of ocean. Now he definitely doubted his earlier reasoning and began to think that they must be out over the Irish Sea. He had visions of losing the entire squadron as, one by one, they ran out of fuel and were forced to bail out. The situation had become desperate.

The Spitfire pilots of the Eagle Squadron, meanwhile, had followed

a different course and, in the belief that they were near their base, began letting down through the murky cloud cover. As the visibility cleared, they sighted a coastline and assumed it was England. It was France and they soon crossed over the harbor at Brest through a terrifying flak barrage. In only a few moments ten Spitfires were lost, shot down or forced down through lack of fuel, with four of the pilots killed and six captured, among them the leader, Gordon Brettell. Another Eagle Spitfire had had to abort after taking off, due to mechanical trouble. Their twelfth Spit crash-landed in France, but the pilot evaded capture and made it safely back to England. Brettell became a prisoner of war in Stalag Luft III and was one of those involved in the "Great Escape." Recaptured, he was one of the fifty prisoners later murdered by the Nazis for his part in the escape attempt.

The situation now seemed hopeless to Brian. Logic seemed of no value and he chose to simply rely on instinct. They would press on.

Shortly after that decision, he heard an all but inaudible crackle in his earphones which then became, "Hello, Brian. Hello, Brian. This is ground control. Are you receiving me? Over." The voice told him that he was still about eighty miles south of base, to fly due north and to carefully watch his fuel. With plenty of altitude, he throttled back to minimum revs and set up for a long, shallow descent towards Bolt Head. They made it with only one pilot running out of fuel and having to bail out short of the coast.

Many years later, the true cause of the Morlaix disaster was discovered: the odd phenomenon we know today as the "jet stream," strange bands of air moving at high speed at altitudes above 20,000 feet, which can sometimes create

unpredicted tailwinds that can propel an aircraft along at 100 mph (or more) faster than its top speed.

The Morlaix mission had produced tragic consequences for the Eagle Squadron pilots and was a sad and inglorious final action on which to depart from the RAF. For Brian Kingcome and his pilots, it so nearly brought an equally disastrous end.

One of the few remaining airworthy Mk I Spitfires, this example underwent an eight-year total restoration which was completed in 2008. It is seen here over Oxfordshire in the English midlands.

DOING IT BY DAY

In 1942, when Brigadier General Ira C. Eaker of the United States Army Air Force stepped down from his C-47 transport plane at Hendon airport in beleaguered Britain, the war news was as bleak as the February weather. Japanese forces had invaded Singapore, their torpedo planes had sunk two major British battleships, the Americans were making a last stand on Bataan, the Allied armies were retreating across the plains of Libya, the Wehrmacht's Panzer tanks were closing in on Stalingrad, and Atlantic shipping losses to the predatory U-boats were frighteningly high. That very week, the warships *Scharnhorst, Gneisenau,* and *Prinz Eugen* had made a dash through the Channel from their vulnerable anchorages in Brest harbor and had reached the safety of a German port. Desperate attempts by the RAF and the Fleet Air Arm had failed to stop them, and critics of air power wanted to know why; recent operations by RAF bombers, restricted by weather, had been relatively modest. British disciples of aerial bombardment were having a hard time.

Two events, however, held some promise of better days to come: one, Eaker's missions were to prepare the way for the arrival of the U.S. Eighth Air Force; two, the RAF's bomber force had a new commander in the redoubtable Air Chief Marshal Arthur T. Harris who had established his headquarters on the hill above High Wycombe.

The early signs, however, were not encouraging. Eight weeks after Eaker's arrival, the two RAF

A U.S. Eighth Air Force Boeing B-17G heavy bomber with members of its crew on their return from a mission to bomb a target in Germany.

Top left: A crumbling Nissen hut at Rougham / Bury St Edmunds; top center and right: 8AF bomber crew members;

below: A section of WWII runway at the Lavenham base of the American 487th Bomb Group, Suffolk.

squadrons then equipped with Avro Lancasters were assigned to attack the great M.A.N. factory in Augsburg, Bavaria, where the U-boats' diesel engines were being made. The concept of mounting a deep-penetration raid in daylight was audacious—as audacious in its way, as the attack, hours later, by Colonel Jimmy Doolittle's carrier-launched force of B-25 Mitchell bombers on targets in Japan. The thinking at High Wycombe was that the new four-engined bombers, flying at low level in two elements of six, stood a good chance of success, and certainly a better chance than the lightly armed Wellingtons, the underpowered Manchesters, and the lumbering Stirlings that formed the bulk of Harris's command, but so much depended on the achievement of surprise. That essential element was lost when, by miscalculation, the first six Lancasters crossed a Luftwaffe fighter field on their passage over France, and four of them were shot down by Me 109s. A fifth was destroyed by flak above the target, as were two of the following element. Only five aircraft, two of which were badly damaged, struggled back to England on that April evening. John Nettleton, their leader, was awarded the Victoria Cross, Britain's highest military distinction. There was no lack of heroism, and no lack of skill (the factory was struck by thirteen one-thousand-pounders), but there was a fatal lack of firepower. The Lancaster's eight machine guns, firing .303 bullets, had been no match for the cannons of the Me 109s.

It so happened, soon after his arrival, that Eaker had visited Harris's headquarters. The two men had worked together in Washington when Harris led a mission there in 1941, and it was as a friend that the American now sought the Englishman's assistance and advice. Eaker was an advocate of precision bombing, essentially in daylight, by well-armed aircraft flying in tight formation, whereas Harris's usual practice was to send his heavy bombers individually by night, making up for the inevitable loss of accuracy by sheer weight of numbers.

After one or two attempts to persuade the American to "come in with us on the night offensive," and a jocular suggestion that Eaker's reluctance was due to the fact that his airmen could only navigate in daylight, Harris accepted Eaker's point. He postponed the formation of a new RAF bomber group (later to emerge as the new Pathfinder Force) to provide the Americans with bases in the Midlands and East Anglia. In addition, the RAF found a fine old building for the Eighth Air Force bomber staff at nearby Daws Hill Lodge, another for the fighter staff at Bushey Hall near Watford and, more importantly, gave the Americans access to a tried and tested nationwide system of communications and control.

An official U.S. record described how the Eighth Air Force was received: "With its Fighter Command guarding the skies by day, the Bomber Command striking the enemy by night, and the Coastal Command sweeping the sea-lanes, the RAF might have taken a condescending attitude towards the advance guard of the Americans whose plans were so large and whose means were apparently so small. The RAF took no such attitude. From the start, their generous and sympathetic interest were the keys that unlocked many problems. 'Tell us what you want,' they said. 'If we have it, it is yours,' 'Whether or not we need it ourselves.' "

The efficient organization of supplies was crucial to the operation, and it was undertaken by one of Eaker's staff, Major Frederick Castle, whose subsquent career as a combat leader was to add a page of glory to the story of the Eighth; USAAF intelligence officers attended briefings and debriefings at RAF bomber fields; technicians took note of the comments made by British airmen on certain operational shortcomings in the early Flying Fortresses and ordered the appropriate improvements. The Americans were welcomed everywhere they went. At a dinner in his honor, Eaker's speech was short and to the point: "We won't do much talking until we've done more flying. We hope that when we leave, you'll be glad we came. Thank you."

In the azure mid-afternoon of August 17, 1942, twelve B-17s of the Ninety-seventh Bomb Group set out from Grafton Underwood on the first Eighth Air Force mission of the war. Taking off at thirty-second intervals, the aircraft climbed up into a sunlit, cloudless sky. Ira Eaker, as commanding general, flew in *Yankee Doodle*, leading the second element of six. The target, appositely, was the railway marshaling yard in Rouen, the city where, five hundred years before, Joan of Arc had died for the liberty of France. Eighteen tons of bombs were dropped from 22,500 feet and all fell on or near the target. None of the bombers (which the Germans identified as Lancasters) suffered more than superficial damage. Their escort of RAF Spitfires, two of which were lost, destroyed two Messerschmitts and claimed five more as "probables." When the B-17s returned to Grafton Underwood at seven o'clock that evening, the first to land was *Yankee Doodle*, as was right and proper. A message from Harris was brought to Ira Eaker: "Yankee Doodle certainly went to town, and can stick yet

another well-earned feather in his cap."

The weather stayed fine and the Ninety-seventh flew three more short-range missions with no losses to the bombers. Then, on August 21, nine B-17s on route to Rotterdam were late for the rendezvous with their fighter escort, and the Spitfires, short of fuel, were obliged to leave them halfway to the target. A recall was broadcast later, but for twenty minutes the German fighter pilots had the bombers to themselves. In the ensuing combat, the Fortress gunners claimed to have destroyed two fighters and to have damaged five, but one straggling bomber, attacked by five Fw 190s, was lucky to escape with one man wounded and another dying. It was a salutary engagement.

Lewis E. Lyle, Commander, 303rd and 379th Bomb Groups, USAAF, on the August 17, 1943, mission to attack the ball-bearing works at Schweinfurt, Germany: "You just went to the target by following the fires."

The Consolidated B-24 Liberators entered the arena on October 9 when the Ninety-third Bomb Group joined the Ninety-seventh in an attack on steel works and locomotive factories in Lille, France. There were a number of "abortives," with bombs dropped in the Channel, and only sixty-nine of 108 bombers reached the primary target. Nevertheless, it was the heaviest raid yet mounted by the Eighth, a distinction that it would hold, for one reason or another, for the next six months. It was also the first time the bombers had tangled with the Luftwaffe in force. As one navigator put it: "Lille was our first real brawl." In over two combats the enemy fighters only succeeded in shooting down four bombers, but

the skill and ferocity demonstrated by the German pilots gave notice of what might be expected in the days to come.

Although enthusiastic claims of over sixty enemy aircraft certainly or probably destroyed were greeted with caution by the debriefing officers, and subsequently reduced to forty-two, the figures still showed that the gunners in the well-named Flying Fortresses could give a good account of themselves.

The flak above the target was described by a Liberator crewman as "the worst I've ever seen." The fact that he was flying his first mission detracted a little from the force of the remark, but ensured its remembrance in the annals of the group.

In November 1942, tactics were still in the process of evolving when, seeking greater accuracy, thirty-one B-17s attacked the U-boat pens at St Nazaire from less than half their normal bombing height. Three of the aircraft were shot down by flak, and twenty-two were damaged. There were no more medium-altitude attacks by heavy bombers. The 305th Bomb Group commander, Colonel Curtis E. LeMay, decided to abandon individual bomb runs: his squadrons would fly in train above the target, and each plane's bombs would be dropped when the leader's load began to fall. Two months later, St Nazaire was once again the target when LeMay's method was employed. The results were encouraging: more bombs fell near the MPI, the mean point of impact of an ideal strike. Bomb-on-the-leader tactics had been tried and proven.

"The enemy must be attacked by day and by night," announced Sir Archibald Sinclair, the British Air Secretary, "so that he may have no respite from the Allied blows, so

Lieutenant Bert Stiles of the Ninety-first Bomb Group, based at Bassingbourn near Cambridge, England, was a student at Colorado College in 1942 when he joined the American Army Air Force. He received his commission in November 1943, and went overseas to Great Britain in March 1944. He was awarded the Air Medal and the Distinguished Flying Cross and flew thirty-five bomber missions. Instead of returning to America when leave was due him, he asked to be transferred to fighters. On November 26, 1944, he shot down an Fw190 and was then killed in the crash of his P-51 Mustang as a result of the combat.

Left: The crew of the B-17 *Buckeye Belle*, 384th Bomb Group at Grafton Underwood in Northamptonshire; below: The memorial to members of the Thirty-Fourth Bomb Group stationed at Mendlesham, England, in WWII.

TO THE AMERICAN AIRMEN
OF THE '34TH', WHO, IN VALOR
GAVE THEIR LIVES TO THE VICTORY
THAT MADE REAL THE CHALLENGE
FOR WORLD PEACE AND UNITY

THE 34TH HEAVY BOMBARDMENT GROUP
A UNIT OF THE UNITED STATES
EIGHTH AIR FORCE
IN WORLD WAR II,
APRIL 1944 TO JUNE 1945
MENDLESHAM AERO-
DROME SUFFOLK

that his defensive resources may be taxed to the utmost limit. But day and night bombing are separate though complementary tasks. Each requires a strategic plan, a tactical execution, and a supporting organization adapted to its special needs. So there has been a division of labour. To one force—the Eighth Bomber Command—has been allocated the task of day bombing. To the other force—our Bomber Command—the task of night bombing. The methods are different, but the aim is the same: to paralyze the armed forces of Germany by disrupting the war economy by which they are sustained."

The civil servant who prepared those phrases for his minister had no need to pull his punches. In the year just passed, bombing policy had changed. The RAF's attacks were no longer restricted to "military targets," and gone were the days when only propaganda leaflets could be dropped on cities. The early German air attacks on Warsaw, Rotterdam, Coventry, and London had shown what could be done, and Britain's mood had hardened. "They have sown the wind," said Air Chief Marshal Harris, "now they will reap the whirlwind."

Initially, there had been little difference in the way the bomber tactics of the Luftwaffe and the RAF evolved. Both had begun with daylight raids—the Germans on what had then seemed a massive scale—both had suffered heavy losses from the other's air defenses, and both had been obliged to seek the cover of the night. It was in the way the opposing forces developed and conducted their night operations that the differences emerged. A major factor was that the German aircraft industry was never able to provide the Luftwaffe with an effective heavy bomber, whereas the British airplane designers, responding

to the RAF's requirement, produced the huge four-engined Stirling, the Handley Page Halifax and, at last, the Avro Lancaster. Then, to find their targets, the German crews depended on visual checkpoints such as estuaries and rivers, or, when bombing through the overcast, by flying along a radio beam transmitted from Europe; the RAF, meanwhile, was developing radar navigation and all-weather methods of pyrotechnic target marking.

The main contrast, however, between the two offensives was in their weight and scale. While the Eighth's day offensive was gathering momentum, and Harris's new heavies flew in growing numbers to pound industrial targets deep inside the Reich, the German raids dwindled until they could be regarded, strategically at least, as of nuisance value only. Although Hitler still had some lethal shots left in his locker—the "little blitz" on London in early 1944, and the "doodlebugs" and rockets that prolonged Britain's ordeal until their launching sites were smashed— from that time on, German factories were trundling out fighters, not bombers, and that was no way to win a war. There can be no doubt that the enemy was forced into this defensive posture by the USAAF's daylight raids.

For the participants—the men who flew the airplanes—there were many differences between a day mission in a Fortress or a Liberator and a night operation in a British bomber. For one thing, the RAF crews tried not to tangle with the night fighters, and used various tactics—electronic countermeasures, spoof attacks, and feints—to put them off the scent. The fliers of the Eighth, on the other hand, deliberately set out to take the fighters on: with the great formations shining in the sunlight and leaving condensation

trails for many miles behind them, they presented a challenge no defending air force could refuse. In this, the USAAF's air divisions could be likened to regiments of cavalry, riding high upon a hillside, silhouetted on the skyline, with guidons fluttering and bugles blowing the charge; "Butch" Harris's men, on the other hand, were more like the infantry, moving through the lines in darkness, with blackened faces and muffled tread.

It was when they reached their targets that the Allied fliers shared a mutual experience. There, the reception was very much the same; it just looked rather different. The crewmen saw ahead of them an apparently impenetrable barrier of flak, standing in their way from the start of the bomb run to the release point and beyond. At night it appeared as a million sparks among the groping searchlights; by day, as a sky full of lumps of dirty cotton. That was what they had to fly through, day or night. There was no point in trying to dodge between the shell bursts: in evading one they might fly into another. Nor was there any chance of dodging, even if they wanted to, once the airplane was committed to the bomb run. From that moment on, it was the man with his thumb on the bomb release button who was in control, and he had eyes only for the aiming point or the lead plane's bomb bay.

However similar the physical experiences over the target were, there was a marked distinction in the human aspect. The crewmen of a USAAF heavy bomber were flying close to other guys they knew: at the controls of the Fortress above their starboard wing was the pilot's buddy; one of the navigator's poker pals was flying in the nose of the airplane on their left; the gunners in the lead ship up ahead shared a billet with their own. When

8AF Bomber Command jacket patches.

any of those aircraft lost a battle with a fighter, or a flak battery scored a lethal hit, there was a personal interest in seeing who got out. Everyone should, of course, be concentrating on his job, but when you knew that Ed was in that ship, and little Virgil from Ohio, you couldn't help but watch and whisper, "Come on, you guys, get the hell out of there!"

At night it was different, and utterly impersonal. No one could identify the men who had just disappeared in a blinding flash of light; no one had a clue who was trapped inside that burning Lancaster making a meteoric arc across the sky. The crew of a night bomber were seven men essentially alone.

Nissen hut living quarters near the runways at Grafton Underwood, Northamptonshire.

AL DEERE

The most famous of the New Zealand pilots in the Battle of Britain was Group Captain Alan C. Deere, who was in continuous action as a Spitfire pilot from the beginning of the war until 1943. By then his official score was twenty-two enemy aircraft destroyed, ten probably destroyed, and eighteen damaged. Of him, Air Chief Marshal Lord Dowding wrote: "Alan Deere must have had an exceptionally efficient Guardian Angel who, even so, must have been hard put to it to extricate his charge from the apparently hopeless predicaments in which he was constantly finding himself."

Deere: "Fastening on to the tail of a yellow-nosed Messerschmitt I fought to bring my guns to bear as the range rapidly decreased, and when the wingspan of the enemy aircraft fitted snugly into the range scale bars of my relector sight, I pressed the firing button. There was an immediate response from my eight Brownings which, to the accompaniment of a slight bucketing from my aircraft, spat a stream of lethal lead targetwards. 'Got you' I muttered to myself as the small dancing yellow flames of exploding De Wilde bullets spattered along the Messerschmitt's fuselage. My exultation was short-lived. Before I could fire another burst two 109s wheeled in behind me. I broke hard into the attack pulling my Spitfire into a climbing, spiralling turn as I did so; a manoeuvre I had discovered in previous combats with 109s to be particularly effective. And it was no less effective now; the Messerschmitts literally 'fell out of the sky' as they stalled in an attempt to follow me.

"I soon found another target. About 3,000 yards directly ahead of me, and at the same level, a Hun was

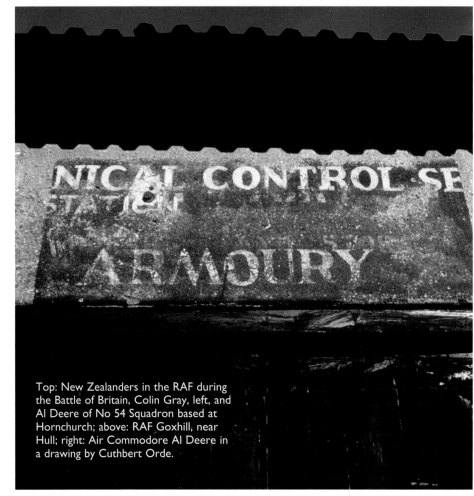

Top: New Zealanders in the RAF during the Battle of Britain, Colin Gray, left, and Al Deere of No 54 Squadron based at Hornchurch; above: RAF Goxhill, near Hull; right: Air Commodore Al Deere in a drawing by Cuthbert Orde.

just completing a turn preparatory to re-entering the fray. He saw me almost immediately and rolled out of his turn towards me so that a head-on attack became inevitable. Using both hands on the control column to steady the aircraft and thus keep my aim steady, I peered through the reflector sight at the rapidly closing enemy aircraft. We opened fire together, and immediately a hail of lead thudded into my Spitfire. One moment the Messerschmitt was a clearly defined shape, its wingman nicely enclosed within the circle of my reflector sight, and the next it was on top of me, a terrifying blur which blotted out the sky ahead. Then we hit.

"The force of the impact pitched me violently forward onto my cockpit harness, the straps of which bit viciously into my shoulders. At the same moment, the control column was snatched abruptly from my gripping fingers by a momentary, but powerful, reversal of elevator load. In a flash it was over; there was clear sky ahead of me, and I was still alive. But smoke and flame were pouring from the engine which began to vibrate, slowly at first but with increasing momentum causing the now regained control column to jump back and forwards in my hand. Hastily I closed the throttle and reached forward to flick off the ignition switches, but before I could do so the engine seized and the airscrew stopped abruptly. I saw with amazement that the blades had been bent almost double with the impact of the collision; the Messerschmitt must have been just that fraction above me as we hit.

"With smoke now pouring into the cockpit I reached blindly forward for the hood release toggle and tugged at it violently. There was no welcoming and expected rush of air to denote that the hood had been jettisoned. Again and again I pulled at the toggle but there was no response. In desper-

ation I turned to the normal release catch and exerting my full strength endeavoured to slide back the hood. It refused to budge; I was trapped. There was only one thing to do; try to keep the aircraft under control and head for the nearby coast. The speed had by now dropped off considerably, and with full backward pressure on the stick I was just able to keep a reasonable gliding altitude. If only I could be lucky enough to hit in open country where there was a small chance that I might get away with it.

"Frantically I peered through the smoke and flame enveloping the engine, seeking with streaming eyes for what lay ahead. There could be no question of turning; I had no idea what damage had been done to the fuselage and the tail of my aircraft, although the mainplanes appeared to be undamaged, and I daren't risk even a small turn at low level, even if I could have seen to turn.

"Through a miasmatic cloud of flame and smoke the ground suddenly appeared ahead of me. The next moment a post flashed past my wing tip and then the aircraft struck the ground and ricocheted into the air again finally returning to earth with a jarring impact, and once again I was jerked forward on to my harness. Fortunately the straps held fast and continued to do so as the aircraft ploughed its way through a succession of splintering posts before finally coming to a halt on the edge of a cornfield. Half blinded by smoke and frantic with fear I tore at my harness release pin. And then with my bare hands wielding the strength of desperation, I battered at the Perspex hood which entombed me. With a splintering crash it finally cracked open, thus enabling me to scramble from the cockpit to the safety of the surrounding field.

"At a safe distance from the aircraft

A Mk Ia Spitfire over the English midlands in 2008.

Crew members of Heinkel He-111 bombers relaxing on their French base before a raid on a target in England.

I sat down to observe the damage to person and property. My hands were cut and bleeding; my eyebrows were singed; both knees were badly bruised; and blood trickled into my mouth from a slightly cut lip. But I was alive! I learned later from the technical officer who examined the wreckage after the fire had been put out, that the seat had broken free from the lower retaining bar thus pivoting upwards, and so throwing my knees against the lower part of the dashboard.

"The aircraft had ploughed a passage through three fields, studded with anti-invasion posts erected to prevent enemy gliders from landing, and bits of aircraft and posts were strewn along the three hundred yards of its path. My Spitfire was now a blazing mass of metal from which a series of explosions denoted that the heat was igniting the unused ammunition, to the consternation of a knot of onlookers who had by now collected at the scene of the crash.

"A woman, whom I had observed coming from a nearby farmhouse, approached me and said, 'I have telephoned Manston airfield and they say that an ambulance and fire engine are already on the way. Won't you come in and have a cup of tea?'

" 'Thank you, I will, but I would prefer something stronger if you've got it.'

" 'Yes, I think there is some whisky in the house. Will that do?'

" 'Yes, thanks, just what the doctor would order. I'm sorry about messing up your fields; let's hope the fire engine gets here before the fire spreads to that field of corn. Incidentally, how far are we from Manston?'

" 'Oh not far, about five miles by road. Your people should be here soon.'

"Turning to a small cluster of the more curious onlookers, who had crept closer to the wreckage, I said, 'I

The original plotting board in the underground Ops Room at RAF Uxbridge, near London's Heathrow airport.

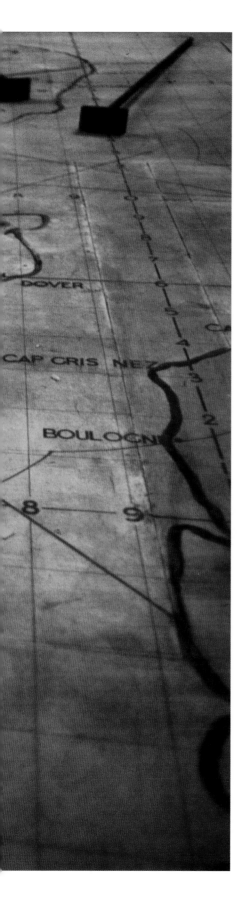

advise you to stand well clear of the aircraft. There is plenty of high-octane fuel in the tanks and an explosion is a distinct possibility.' This remark had an immediate effect and they hastily retreated to a safe distance.

"Before long, an anxious M.O. arrived with the ambulance and examined me cursorily before conveying me back to Manston. The squadron had returned to Rochford by the time I arrived so I was forced to spend the night there. If the doctor had had his way I would have been bedded down in the station sick quarters, but after a certain amount of persuasive talk on my part he released me to return to the mess. The following morning saw me airborne in a Tiger Moth trainer, accompanied by Flying Officer Ben Bowring, a prewar rugger compatriot, and headed for Rochford with thoughts of a couple of days off. There was to be no respite, however. 'Prof's' first words on seeing me were: 'Thank heavens you're back, Al. Are you fit to fly?'

" 'Reluctantly, yes,' I answered. 'A bit shaken I must admit. Why the urgent note in your voice?'

" 'Well, we are damned short of pilots. Perhaps you haven't been told yet, but we lost two of your chaps in that show yesterday, both presumed killed.' "

" 'If we are ordered off again before dusk the Controller says we are to land back at Hornchurch,' said 'Prof' addressing a tired, but happy assembly of 54 [Squadron] pilots lounging on the grass near their parked Spitfires.

" 'I've had enough today,' said Colin [Gray]. I reckon the Huns have too. Perhaps they will let us return in peace to Hornchurch. I'm just dying for a beer, a good meal and bed.'

"His hopes were not to be realized. Hardly were the words uttered when the warning bell, the signal to the ground crews that a scramble had been ordered, was rung by the telephone orderly who could be seen running towards 'Prof' with instructions from the Controller. With one accord nine Spitfires, all that remained serviceable, roared into life and, with pilots impatiently waving the guiding airmen away from the wing tips, they taxied towards the takeoff point soon to be airborne and lost to view as the formation climbed at full throttle towards Dover.

" 'Hornet Leader from Control. Make angels 20,000 feet over Dover.' Ronald Adam's voice floated over the R/T, unruffled and as precise as ever despite the hectic day the Controllers must have had in the Operations Room.

" 'Hornet Leader to Control; your message received. What's the form?'

" 'Seventy plus aircraft, now in mid-Channel. Should make landfall between Dungeness and Dover. You are to engage the escort fighters. Is this understood?'

" 'Hornet Leader to Control, understood.'

"That's a new one,' I thought. The first time we've been given specific orders to engage the escort fighters; must enquire when I get down what it is all about.

"Steadily the squadron climbed towards the south coast until at 25,000 feet we leveled out and turned southeast in the direction of the approaching enemy. Bitter experience of being jumped from above had taught us to add on at least 5,000 feet to the inaccurate radar heights passed over the R/T. The wisdom of this was now apparent. As we swept in a wide arc from the south towards the now plainly visible enemy formation, it was clear that there would be little height advantage over the top escort which formed

The wreck of a Messerschmitt
Bf109 fighter brought down
by RAF aircraft over southern
England in 1940; far right: A
Heinkel He-111 bomber over
the English countryside, 1940.

an unbroken chain down to the bombers tucked tightly together some 7,000 feet below. 'If we can manage to draw off some of these escort fighters,' I thought, 'some lucky chaps are going to have a wonderful picnic. Those are Me 110s acting as bombers.' The Me 110 was a particularly vulnerable aircraft and a dream target when on a formation bombing mission, as they were then precluded from forming a defensive circle, their normal tactic when attacked and one against which there was no real answer.

"Prof's manoeuvre to the south brought us in behind the enemy fighters which were completely taken by surprise. We were in among them before they took any action, and two 109s were destroyed in the first attack. Breaking upwards from this attack, I soon found myself another target; a 109 dived underneath me and headed eastwards towards France. I realized that if he spotted me the Hun pilot would immediately go into a steep dive, in which the Messerschmitt was superior to the Spitfire, and there would be little hope of catching him. My tactic was therefore to stay just below his height and in the blind spot formed by the tail unit of his aircraft to exploit to the maximum the bad rearwards visibility of the Messerschmitt. A long stern chase ensued and the shores of England were soon far behind us as the enemy pilot rapidly lost height towards home.

"At about 5,000 feet, and when I was almost in range to fire, the Messerschmitt entered a thin layer of cloud and was lost to view momentarily. So intent was I on the chase that I hadn't realized that we had crossed the Channel. It was only when I broke through the cloud behind the Hun that I saw with horror the coast of France was directly below. The Messerschmitt was still ahead—he obviously hadn't

seen me—and now [was] steepening his dive towards an airfield to our left. I dared not wait any longer to open fire and, although not quite in range, I pressed the firing button. The Hun's reaction was to stand his aircraft practically on its nose and dive vertically towards the airfield which I now recognized as Calais / Marck! An omen, alas, for I again met more enemy than I had bargained for; the circuit was infested with 109s, two of which detached themselves and turned to cut me off as, with throttle wide open, I headed home at sea level.

"The 109s were winning the race, having the shorter distance to go, and I waited for the first attack to develop. A most unpleasant prospect, and the liklihood of more joining in made it more so; and me so far from our coast. At all costs, I reasoned, I must try and keep them both in view while at the same time making headway towards England. It wasn't going to be easy; the 109s had now split, one on either side of me. There was no point in just staying to fight, I was on the run and intended to keep it that way if I could.

"Down came the first one to the attack; around went my Spitfire in a vicious turn in his direction causing him to break without firing. In came the number two; around the other way I went and he too broke without firing. And so it went on. I knew that before long they would bring their guns to bear as with each succeeding attack I became more tired, and they more skilful. At last, one of them found his mark; bullets riddled my aircraft shattering the instrument panel and canopy. It was a miracle that I wasn't hit, the armour plate behind my seat no doubt deflecting a great number of bullets. Again and again they came at me; again and again I turned into the attack, but still the bullets, fortunately no cannon shells, found their target

Jonathan Whaley at the controls of this restored Mk I Spitfire fighter.

until eventually the now vibrating engine confirmed my worst fears. The oil tank had been punctured; a steady stream flowed over the cowlings and on to the windscreen, partly obscuring my vision ahead. How long would it keep going, I wondered. There was no longer any point in turning into each attack; I must get nearer to England and the only way to achieve this was to head straight for the now faintly visible Dover cliffs, while at the same time presenting as difficult a target as possible. This I achieved by kicking violently on first one rudder and then on the other, alternatively shoving the stick from side to side to introduce a slipping effect into the violently yawing aircraft. Thus, I offered a none too easy shot to the attackers.

"At long last the beckoning white of the Dover cliffs lay just ahead. The nearness of the coastline spelled danger to the Hun pilots who disengaged and turned tail for home, displaying a discretion I would do well to observe in future.

"In one backward movement of the control column, I increased my height to about 1,500 feet, using my forward speed to effect the manoeuvre, and throttling back I peered anxiously at my oil gauges. Both were shattered. As a precautionary measure I jettisoned my splintered hood. It was as well that I did for a matter of seconds later the engine burst into flames despite the fact that I had now throttled fully back, having decided to make a forced landing in the immediate vicinity.

"I wasted no time in making a decision to abandon the aircraft, it was the only safe way of escape in the circumstances. I rolled the aircraft onto its back—as recommended by Johnny Allen who had successfully used this manoeuvre when he baled [sic] out during Dunkirk—having first released my Sutton harness, and pushed

the control column hard forward. Immediately I shot out of my seat only to be caught by my parachute fouling some part of the cockpit when I was almost clear of the aircraft. Before I could get back into the aircraft, which I tried to do, the nose of the aircraft dropped alarmingly and it was then I realized that I hadn't put the actuating trimmer fully forward, a necessary precaution when attempting to bale [sic] out of an inverted aircraft as it tends to keep the nose up. Frantically I struggled to get free, but the increasing airflow over the cockpit was forcing me backwards against the fuselage. With the aircraft almost vertical, and the ground alarmingly close, I at last broke loose and was hurled backwards against the tailplane which struck my right wrist a crushing blow. The parachute responded immediately to the pull of the rip cord, and a matter of seconds later I hit the ground not a hundred yards from where my burning *Kiwi* had exploded in a sheet of flame.

"I suffered no further injury on landing and was in the process of disentangling myself from the parachute harness when two airmen appeared unexpectedly on the scene.

" 'Where did you two spring from?' I enquired.

" 'We are on our way to Kenley,' answered one of the airmen. 'I am an ambulance driver and he's a nursing orderly. We saw your aircraft crash and were on our way to see what we could do when we saw you in this field. Can we do anything? The ambulance is just beyond that clump of trees over there.'

" 'Yes, you can give me a lift.' "

RAF fighter pilots muscle a Spitfire of their squadron from a maintenance facility in December 1942.

A cannon-armed Mk IX ready for takeoff at RAF Duxford in Cambridgeshire.

JACK ILFREY

Ilfrey: "I became a natural-born flier through instinct. Both of my parents were somewhat adventurous. My father was a World War I fighter pilot and instructor. After the war, he joined the Texas National Guard. My first ride in an airplane, as a very young kid, was strapped on my mother's lap in a Jenny while my father flew it. He also did some motorcycle, speedboat, and auto racing, while I tagged along, reveling in the thrill of it all. I did some of the same as a teenager. Even though some of us were considered to be natural-born fliers, we still had to learn to be masters of our aircraft."

November 20, 1944. Captain Jack Ilfrey was leading five P-51D Mustang fighters of the 20th Fighter Group, Eighth U.S. Army Air Force, to rendezvous with a pair of F-5A [P-38] photo reconnaissance aircraft. The Mustangs were going to cover the F-5As whose job that day was to photograph Berlin and the surrounding area.

The weather conditions were relatively good. There was about seven-tenths cloud cover. The flak, thus far, had been only light. When the F-5s finished their photography, they headed southwest over the Autobahn towards Magdeburg. As they went they attracted more intense flak. They were also required to photograph the Bonn area, where American bombers had attacked airfields and synthetic oil facilities. Before reaching Bonn, however, the F-5s radioed that they were low on both fuel and film and were going to head back to their base. By this time the weather had deteriorated, with the overcast becoming solid. Only the occasional glimpse of the earth appeared.

Top left: 20th Fighter Group pilot Jack Ilfrey with his ground crew at Kings Cliffe; bottom left: The 8AF shoulder patch; above: Captain Ilfrey with his P-51D Mustang, *Happy Jack's Go-Buggy*.

A P-51D Mustang at RAF Martlesham Heath
Suffolk, in 1944.

After carrying out their required duties on escort missions, it had become standard practice for the Mustang pilots of the 20th Fighter Group to head down to the deck to locate and shoot up any targets of opportunity on the way back to their Kings Cliffe base. After several months of flying operations with the Mustangs, the pilots of the group had come to greatly appreciate this finest of American fighter types. "The P-51s made us feel like hunters in the skies over Germany. Our morale was high during ground strafing, chasing, or evading their fighters, or just firing the guns. We got an adrenalin high."

The Mustangs spiraled down through a hole in the cloud cover and soon found an abundance of trucks, tanks, and other vehicles heading for the front lines. The American fighters were heading northwest, continuing under the massive weather front and busying themselves shooting at the various enemy targets that presented themselves. At one point Ilfrey realized that he was not quite sure where his little group was while on their way back to England. He told the other pilots to form on him and they would set course for home.

They had expended a lot of ammunition and most of their fuel by this time. It was a little after four in the afternoon and was getting dark fairly early there in the late autumn. Ilfrey set his course but was thinking that, with relatively little fuel remaining, they might have to land in France or Belgium. He decided they would fly low, beneath the weather front, as a stream of bombers might also be heading back to England through the overcast. Ilfrey: "We were in a good, tight formation heading back. My wingman, Duane Kelso, radioed that he been hit by flak and was losing power. We were at around 700 feet in poor

Above and right: Restored Mustang fighters at the Flying Legends air show, Duxford in Cambridgeshire, England.

visibility when I happened to see a clear stretch which appeared to be a small emergency strip surrounded by trees. There were a few bombed-out buildings and a few wrecked aircraft scattered around. I pointed out the strip and told Kelso to try for it, and that I would try to cover him. Knowing we were almost out of ammunition and very low on fuel, I told the other pilots that they were on their own. They all made it okay to Belgium."

Ilfrey then instructed Kelso to use his own judgment about whether to try a wheels-down landing and, if he did decide to do so and thought that Ilfrey could make it in there as well, to give him a "thumbs-up" signal as he circled the strip. All the while both Ilrey and Kelso were being fired on from the ground. Under that heavy ground fire, Kelso approached the short strip and made a rather hairy landing with wheels down, stopping just short of the edge of the trees. He quickly left

the Mustang, observed by Ilfrey who continued to attract the ground fire while circling the little patch. As Ilfrey circled above the trees, Kelso flashed a wide grin and gave his leader the thumbs-up signal.

Ilfrey: "I must have been out of my mind, but the thought of not going in never occurred to me. He was a good pilot, and excellent wingman, and would have followed me anywhere, and I couldn't help feeling very close to him at that moment. Flashing through my mind was how Art Heiden and Jesse Carpenter had tried to pick me up when I had been shot down on June 13th, but couldn't because of the trees and the glider barriers where I had come down, and of their thoughts when they had to leave me there deep in enemy-occupied territory. Friendships forged in combat are never forgotten."

Impetuously, Jack Ilfrey lowered his wheels and flaps and took his Mustang,

Happy Jack's Go-Buggy, in for an equally hair-raising landing on the little strip. The Germans in the area were now firing on Kelso's plane and Kelso quickly put 100 yards between himself and his former mount. He ran to the end of the strip where he believed Ilfrey would stop and turn around, ready for an immediate takeoff, regardless of wind direction.

Ilfrey: "God, what a hairy landing, dodging holes, muddy as hell, but the *Go-Buggy* made it. I taxied the short distance up to Kelso, set the brakes, and jumped out on the wing. I took off my 'chute and dinghy and threw them away. Kelso got in and sat in what now was just a bucket seat lowered all the way down. We immediately discovered that four legs were not going to fit in the space and allow me full rudder control, so I stood up and he crossed his legs under him and I sat on them. There was no time to try other positions or adjust the seat and shoul-

der harness. I nearly scalped myself trying to close the canopy. Thank God it was a 'D' [with a large bubble canopy]. So, there I was . . . head and neck bent down, knees almost up to my chin. As I closed the canopy and turned the P-51 to start the takeoff roll, we were well aware that ground troops were firing at us and we were very tense. I yelled back at Kelso, 'Don't get an erection or it'll push me out of here.' ''

Ilfrey thought they were not going to clear the trees. He threw down more flaps and the Mustang barely pulled up over them. Fortunately, it had been light in fuel and ammunition. They made the short flight to Brussels and yet another wild and difficult landing. That night they celebrated.

The next morning, hungover and still without a parachute and dinghy, Ilfrey brought the *Go-Buggy* back to Kings Cliffe and Kelso arrived a few days later by transport. Colonel Rau, the group commander, gave Ilfrey hell

for "pulling a trick like that," jeopardizing himself and his aircraft.

In all the ensuing years, Jack Ilfrey did not see or hear from Duane Kelso.

Jack Ilfrey: "I always associated the German pilot in his aircraft as just 'the aircraft trying to shoot me down.' However, the beast in me was always there, making every effort to stay alive. I can remember saying to myself 'Ha ha, you son of a bitch, I gotcha.' The after feelings were various—remorse, guilt, elation, joy . . . victorious. I think my worst experience along this line was the day my flight of four P-38s got jumped in North Africa. I saw my wingman firing at one, while two enemy aircraft were coming in on him. It was like they were right in front of my eyes, but out of my range. I did my damnedest to get over to help him, but saw him hit the silk, and I suddenly had to fight for my life. I got two Fws, but lost the other three in my flight. A most

awful feeling of helplessness. There was a bond between us that most people can never attain in a lifetime . . . somewhat akin to love of your fellow man, I guess. Then there were the feelings in reverse, when my flight leader literally saved my life when I was badly shot up. I find all this hard to explain.''

Ilfrey: ''. . . the changeover from P-38s to P-51s had not been entirely completed and I had a lot of work to do. All the P-38s and P-47s in the Eighth Air Force were being transferred to the Ninth and were being used for tactical purposes in support of the ground troops on the Continent. All fighter groups in the Eighth Air Force were being equipped with new P-51s, and the Mustang was proving to be a better all-around airplane than the P-38 for long range escort in our strategic work. Our morale went up, our victories went up, and our losses went down.

"Added to the superior qualities of the P-51 were the 'G' suit, or anti-blackout suit, and the new British gyroscopic gun sight. These things gave us a better feeling of aggressiveness because whereas we were limited in the P-38s in diving characteristics and manoeuvring, the P-51 could do more things. I had no more fear of flying around Berlin than I used to around Los Angeles with several of my buddies, of course; but we were all probably wishing it was Los Angeles.

"The anti-blackout suit kept the pilots from blacking out when exceptional gravitational pull was encountered, such as pulling out of a dive or short and qjuick turns. A human body can only stand from three to four Gs, that is, three to four times the weight of your body pulling against you before blacking out, which occurs when all the blood drains from the head causing temporary blindness.

"The G suit was a zipped-on suit, which had a large rubber bladder around the abdomen and legs, forcing the blood to stay in the head.

"With this invention, the pilot could withstand as many Gs as the airplane could, and in the case of a P-51 this was up to nine or ten Gs; more than that and the wings would have probably been pulled off. We wouldn't be caught without our G suit on.

"We nicknamed our new gyroscopic sight the 'No-Miss-Em' gun sight. It took care of all deflection and skid and when it was properly lined up, you just pulled the trigger and got yourself a German airplane . . . or so it says here.

"Cy Wilson was our new group commander. I had known Cy back in the States and he was very eager to go overseas. So when an order came to ship out five second lieutenants, he put down the names of four lieutenants and himself on the order. He drew a 'dud'—Iceland—and after almost a

year there he came to England and took over our group. Cy helped me a lot with the duties of squadron commander. He was a well-liked CO and he'd never ask anyone to do anything he wouldn't do. When it came to flying and leading missions, Cy was tops. He had to be the first to shoot at anything, and he was a great help to our morale.

"I soon found out being squadron commander involved much more responsibility than I had anticipated. I had always felt when I had troubles, I had no one to blame but myself. Now I had 250 men who could get me into trouble and get me into trouble they did—twenty-four hours a day. I was also responsible for all of the squadron's equipment, and it seemed funny to write off lost airplanes and other material running into hundreds of thousands of dollars. I was lucky in having a good 'exec,' a ground officer, and a good first sergeant. I was luckier still in having an outfit with good spirit and a high morale. We were bothered very little with the so-called officer caste system. After all, the pilots were the ones in the fighter squadron who went out and got shot at and the enlisted men respected them for that, if nothing else. The ground crews took great pride in their ships and the pilots. Each airplane had one pilot assigned to it and a ground crew consisting of a crew chief (technical sergeant), and assistant crew chief, a radio maintenance man, and an armorer who took care of the guns and gun camera.

"The airplanes were divided into four flights for maintenance and we had a weekly contest among our flights. The one who had the most airplanes in commission and the greatest number of combat hours flown for the week were usually given a beer 'bust' by the pilots who flew the planes in the winning flight.

"Usually at the end of each month

the pilots would give a beer 'bust' for the men in the squadron, and we tried to have these beer 'busts' on nights when we knew there would be no flying next day and the men wouldn't have to get up early and get the ships ready for flight. Shortly after supper all of us would gather in the group briefing room and go over everything that had taken place during the month. Larkin, our intelligence officer, would describe the nature of all the missions the pilots had flown. Combat films from the gun cameras would be shown with explanation from the pilots. If one of the flyers had had an interesting encounter with the Jerries, he would tell about it. After all questions were answered, we would gather in the hangar for the 'blowing of the suds.' There would be lots of singing, jokes cracked, and a few individual pantomimes, and we'd introduce the new pilots.

"Maybe we were lenient in the Air Corps but whatever our attitude was I think it helped to bring about a better means to an end. Whenever I heard any griping about food and living conditions I always reminded the men they were better off than most of the other boys scattered all over the world. They had places to go and things to do, It wasn't like home, of course, but it wasn't Africa, or sleeping in tents in Italy, or fighting in the South Pacific. We all had a hell of a lot to be grateful for in England.

"The fighter squadron's morale was always higher than in the bomber squadrons. We did not have death brought so close to home as the bombers did. When a fighter was lost or shot down, he just failed to come home. He was missing to the men. But many times crippled bombers came back to base with one or more dead on board, and the men at base got a firsthand view of death. Their buddies were not just missing with hopes of still

An 8AF fighter station Ops Room in WWII England.

A magnificently restored P-51D Mustang fighter in a postwar livery.

being alive. They were right there— dead.

"Cy Wilson was a great one for ground strafing. He literally ate it up. All of us boys used to love to follow him. He had such a good knack for finding locomotives and other excellent targets to strafe. Cy always flew with a big cigar in his mouth, à la Churchill, and I think the only time he ever took it out was when he was flying at high alititudes and had to wear his oxygen mask.

"The last time I saw Cy he had a cigar in his mouth, but I'm sure he wasn't smoking it. He had just baled [sic] out into the North Sea, off the Danish coast, and was sitting in his dinghy, waving at us. We had been strafing an airdrome on the West Danish coast, and Cy had been hit. He managed to fly out to sea several miles before ditching his ship.

"We tried to get Air Sea Rescue to pick him up but we were almost 400

miles from the English coast, which was out of the operating limit of Air Sea Rescue. We hated to leave Cy there in his dinghy, but later we heard that he was a prisoner of the Germans and still later, after V-E Day, he finally came back to the group.

"On long trips of four or five hours or even longer, it often became necessary to relieve one's self. All fighter planes were equipped with a relief tube, but being strapped down tight and at 30,000 feet, with all the heavy clothing on, oxygen mask, helmet, 'G' suit, etc., it was quite a feat if one was able to

successfully complete this manoeuvre without mishap. I'll never forget one mission when I was deep in Germany and it became quite necessary to relieve myself. About halfway through, the tube, being stopped up, became full and I was left holding it, wondering what to do next. I decided to empty it on the floor by my feet, and then I repeated the process all over. I had just gotten through when someone yelled we were being jumped by the Jerries. In evading, I applied some negative pressure to the controls, causing all the urine on the floor to shoot upwards over my front windshield.

When the warm urine hit the very cold glass at 30,000 feet, it froze over solid, blanking out my vision. I frantically tore off my gloves and scraped furiously with my fingers and made enough clear space on the glass so I could see out the front a little. And there I was at 30,000 feet with a fogged-up, urinated windshield. And what did I do . . .''

The Mustang, with its ability to go all the way to the deepest targets with the bombers of the Eighth Air Force assured the ultimate success of the Allied bombing offensive against the Germans.

Squadron Leader Jack Currie flew a Lancaster bomber with No 12 Squadron from RAF Wickenby in Lincolnshire as a Sergeant Pilot.

JACK CURRIE

Many of her crews owe their lives to the strength and power of the RAF's Avro Lancaster bomber. One such crew was that of my late friend and former coauthor, Squadron Leader Jack Currie. Currie: "Hamburg had taken a terrible pounding while we were enjoying our first leave from Wickenby at the end of July. We returned in time to help deliver the final blow on 2nd August. We started DV190 *Baker Two's* engines at 11:30 p.m. and took off twenty minutes later. We circled [the] base on the

climb, and emerged into a clear sky at about 9,000 feet, setting course for Mablethorpe twenty-five minutes after midnight. An hour and ten minutes later we were thirty miles west of Heligoland and in trouble. One port engine was giving no power, the air speed indicator had iced up, and the 19,000 feet of altitude that we had struggled to attain were steadily slipping away. Paths became more difficult to find between the towering thunderclouds that had built up over the North Sea, and whenever the turbulent masses closed about us, *Baker Two* took on more ice and fell another

couple of hundred feet.

"Johnny Walker left the cabin and crawled aft. The Command's new tactic to confuse the enemy radar was the use of 'window,' thin strips of metal foil, and Walker's chilly task was to drop them through the flare chute in the dark and shaking fuselage. Fairbairn left his radio compartment to assist, remarking as he went, with his usual regard for accuracy, that ice on the aerials had increased their diameter from three-sixteenths of an inch to one and a half inches, and was still growing.

"We plunged on southeast for thirty minutes, as hail beat harshly on the canopy, and mauve light flickered about the aerials and front guns. Vivid stabs of lightning opened sudden gorges in the sky, then swirling vapor wrapped us round again. I felt the ice begin to grip the aircraft, now losing height more rapidly. I spoke to the navigator. 'Where are we, Jimmy?'

"'Should be about twenty miles south of the target, but I haven't had a fix for some time. Can you see any flares?'

"'Can't see anything but cumulonimbus.'

"The bombs fell into the storm from 14,000 feet. *Baker Two* leaped at their release and settled into a slow and lurching climb. At 18,000 feet we broke into a shaft of clear air as lightning played among the anvil-headed clouds. Then the guns found us, and the aircraft shook and rattled as the shells burst close. As I turned to miss them, the cloud enveloped us again, and now its icy grip became like iron. Within seconds, the thirty-ton bomber was a toy for the storm to play with, the wheel locked, immobile as a rock. *Baker Two* was out of my control.

"I could see nothing through the window, nothing but a blue infernal glow. I heard no engines, only roaring wind and savage thunderclaps. For the first time in the air, I felt impotence and, with that, a sudden prick of panic. There was nothing I could do—and yet surely I must do something. I held the wheel, watched the instruments, and waited for a clue to action. The instruments belied each other: no airspeed, but climbing fast.

"I felt the stall. The harness straps were pressing hard on my shoulders, my legs were light, loose objects fell about the cabin. Was I hanging in my harness upside down, or was the aircraft falling faster than my weight? I tried to reject the evidence of the whirling gyro-controlled instruments

and to believe the others, which showed nose down, a spin to port, and mounting speed. The ASI had left its ice-bound stop, and was swinging round the dial a second time.

"'Pilot to crew, prepare to abandon aircraft—prepare to abandon.'

"I tried to judge the rate of our descent, and chose 8,000 feet as the height where I must tell the crew to jump. They had to get the hatches open and push themselves into the roaring slipstream, and still leave time for me to follow, before we fell too low to give the silken canopies time to open.

"I don't know whether *Baker Two* or I recovered from the spin, but now there was only the tearing rush of wind, and the steady movement clockwise of the ASI. The needle made a second circuit of the dial, and verged upon the limit of its travel at 400 miles per hour. If the Pitot head were free of ice, so might be the elevators; I pulled back on the wheel with all my strength, as the altimeter read 10,000 feet. At 9,000 feet the wheel jerked violently in my hands, still I pulled and slowly felt my weight increase, and press into the seat, as the diving angle decreased. Briefly, we emerged below the cloud base, and shot up into it again as I struggled with the wheel.

"At last, I found a level attitude at 8,000 feet, and brought the ASI back into the realm of reason. But there was something badly wrong: with the wheel which, although answering my back and forward pressures to climb or dive, wagged loosely left and right without response from either aileron to bank or turn. I wondered if the control cables had snapped—that might have been the violent tremor of the wheel. I pushed the rudders alternately, and *Baker Two* yawed gently in reply.

"'Okay, I've got some control now. Let's have an intercom check—rear

A still from the film *The Dam Busters*, showing Robert Shaw, left, and Richard Todd at the controls of an RAF Lancaster bomber.

An Avro Lancaster bomber is serviced on its dispersal during the Second World War.

gunner?'

" 'No reply from Charlie Lanham.

" 'Mid-upper?'

" 'Mid-upper okay, skipper.'

" 'Engineer?'

" 'No answer from Johnny Walker.'

" 'Wireless operator?'

" 'Wireless operator, strength nine.'

" 'Any idea what's happened to Johnny?'

" 'Last time I saw him, we were both floating up and down the fuselage like a brace of pheasants on the glorious twelfth.'

" 'Okay, go back and see if you can find him. And check the rear gunner, too.'

" 'Wireless op going off intercom.'

"Fairbairn's microphone clicked off, and I continued with the roll call.

" 'Navigator?'

" 'Navigator loud and clear.'

" 'Bomb aimer?'

" 'Bomb aimer Okay, skip.'

"Cassidy could hardly wait for the bomb aimer to reply before he called.

" 'What course are you on?'

"I spun the compass dial. '210 magnetic.'

" 'You're heading straight for Bremen. Turn on to 330.'

" '330. I'll try.'

" 'Mid-upper to skipper. A bloody great piece of your starboard wing's missing—did you know?'

" 'Thanks, George.'

"So that was it. Both ailerons had been torn off in that screaming, spinning dive. I pushed the starboard rudder, and *Baker Two* veered right for a few degrees, wings level, then swung back as I released the pressure on the rudder. I tried again, held the pressure on, and pulled the wheel back slightly. A slow, slithering turn developed. Halfway round, I remembered the rotary potential of the engines—the port outer, free of ice, was running smoothly. Playing with the throttle, I

let the Merlin bring the port wing up, and *Baker Two* settled into a steady, balanced turn.

"A familiar 'puff puff' in my earphones indicated that Fairbairn was checking his microphone before venturing an utterance.

" 'Wireless op here, Jack. I can't find any sign of Johnny, I'm afraid. The main door's open—he might have fallen out. Or jumped. There's a terrible mess down here—"window" all over the place. The rear gunner's in his turret.'

"Myring chimed in from the nose compartment. 'I'll have a look for the engineer, skip. I want to go to the Elsan, anyway.'

" 'Go ahead, Larry. Better get back to your set, Charlie. Pilot to rear gunner?'

" 'Rear gunner, Jack.'

" 'Where were you?'

" 'I got out to find my 'chute. I sat down on the doorstep while you were bringing her down. The whole kite was covered in St Elmo's Fire—ice all over the wings—really a marvelous sight.'

" 'I'm glad you enjoyed it. Did you see anything of the engineer?'

" 'You can't see anything in the fuselage. There's "window" and stuff everywhere. Shall I . . .'

"Protheroe interrupted.

" 'Mid-upper to skipper.'

" 'Go ahead, George.'

" 'I thought the rear gunner ought to know—I shan't be able to fire my guns. The interrupter gear's gone unserviceable. I think something broke off in the spin. Shall I get out and look for Johnny?'

" 'No. Leave that to Larry. Stay in the turret and keep your eyes peeled.'

" 'Wireless op here, Jack. I've been checking the external aerials, and there aren't any. I guess they blew off.'

" 'Bad luck.'

"I flew on, holding *Baker Two* just below the cloud base, at 8,000 feet.

The Joe McCarthy crew, McCarthy center, of No 617 Squadron, RAF, photographed at RAF Scampton near Lincoln. McCarthy, the only American on the famous "Dam Busters" raid, piloted one of the nineteen Lancasters that took part in the attack on the Ruhr dams in May 1943. In the raid, eight of the bombers were shot down or crashed, with fifty-three aircrew killed. Two of the three dams bombed were breached.

An RAF bomber pilot at the controls of an Avro Lancaster in WWII; right: RAF Bomber crew names and units "smoked" on the ceiling of the Eagle Pub in Cambridge in WWII.

When Myring called from the fuselage, he was panting, and I could hear the sound of the slipstream behind his voice. 'I've found the engineer, skip. Buried in bloody "window." He's out cold—I think he banged his nut.'

" 'Is he on oxygen?'

" 'Yep. That's why I don't want to take his helmet off. I'm going to put him on the rest bed. I'll be off intercom for a few minutes.'

" 'Right.'

"We crossed the coast near Bremerhaven at ten minutes before three. Ten minutes later, a searchlight waved towards us from the right, groped closer, and swept the starboard wing. Two more lights from straight below joined the first, and crept along its beam to find us. The flashing stars of flak began to twinkle round us, and I played what evasive games I could with engines, rudders, and elevators. I looked for clouds, but they had disappeared. I spoke to Jimmy.

" 'We're in some defences, Nav.'

" 'Ah, good. Oh, Jack, that'll be Heligoland. I've been waiting for a fix. Let me know when it's right underneath, will you?'

" 'Oh, sure.'

"But now, miraculously, the flak dwindled, and the last two searchlight beams climbed higher up the ladder of the first. I looked up, and there on the port beam, 5,000 feet above us, cruised another Lancaster, majestic, straight and level. The searchlights settled on her, the twinkling flak shells clustered, but she passed on oblivious.

" 'Mid-upper here, skipper. What'd you think of that bugger at ten o'clock high? They must all be asleep!'

"I was glad when another drift of cloud hid the sacrifice from my view. The feeling came that *Baker Two* and we were leading charmed lives that August night, and it was with a degree of confident abandon that, five minutes later, I threw her into steep corkscrew

turns to evade a prowling fighter.

"At 3:30 we turned west-south-west, with 400 miles to go for Mablethorpe. I began to consider how I might make a landing. I had heard no precedent for a Lancaster landing without aileron control, but in my present mood I couldn't think it impracticable, not that night. Larry shattered my euphoria when he returned from nursing Johnny. Crouching beside me, his eyes squinting with alarm, he growled: 'Cripes, Jack, we're bloody short of petrol. These tanks are damn near empty. We'll never make the coast.'

" 'They should be half full. How's Johnny?'

" 'He's conscious but I reckon he's got concussion.'

" 'Pilot to engineer. I need you here to check the fuel. Go and give him a hand, will you, Larry?

"Walker reached the cabin, white-faced and pale-lipped, but with enough sense to get the true readings from the

fuel gauges. Charlie Lanham cackled from the rear turret, 'Duff gen, Myring!'

"Larry crept down into the nose, muttering. Walker was slumped against the starboard cabin window, fumbling at the intercom switch on his mask. I leaned over to turn it off for him, and looked into his eyes. They seemed unfocused, and his face was drained of blood. I told him to go back to the rest bed, but he didn't move, and the wireless operator had to take him aft. When Fairbairn reported that he had made the engineer comfortable, and checked that he was breathing oxygen, Lanham's voice came through my headphones.

" 'Pilot from rear gunner. Do you reckon we're clear of fighters?'

" 'I don't know. I should think so. Why?'

" 'I'll come up and take Johnny's place. Give you a hand.'

"It crossed my mind that he might be feeling lonely in the cold extremity

of *Baker Two's* tail end, or that he had decided that I could use some close moral support. Either way it would be good to have him by my side.

" 'Okay rear gunner. You're clear to leave the turret.'

"Lanham appeared in the cabin a few minutes later, and perched on the engineer's bench seat. Crawling up the fuselage in his heavy suit had brought him out in a sweat. He wiped the back of his gauntlet across his face, then folded his arms and stared ahead into the darkness. His gravely alert expression was exactly suited to the situation, but it made me want to make him laugh. I nudged him with my elbow, and waggled the useless control wheel loosely with my fingertips. I spun it round from left to right, and back again, grinning at Lanham. He looked worried for a moment, staring at the wheel and back at me, then I saw the gleam of his teeth as he laughed. There really wasn't much to laugh about, but the

atmosphere was getting too serious; it needed some of the gravity taken out of it. Lanham settled himself more comfortably and passed me a pellet of chewing gum. He stayed beside me for an hour or so while *Baker Two* flew on westward, sometimes slideslipping a little when I picked up a wandering wing too harshly with the rudders, but on the whole making good her course.

"High above the Lincolnshire coast I brought the speed back, put the wheels down, and tried a rate-one ninety-degree turn to port. I couldn't get any flap down—presumably another system had fractured there—and that meant that I must make a long downwind leg, a shallow approach, and add ten mph to the landing speed. I practiced it at 4,000 feet, and brought *Baker Two* to the point of the stall. The rudder control was good, but I couldn't manipulate the throttles fast enough to keep the wings level. It would have to be a very straight approach.

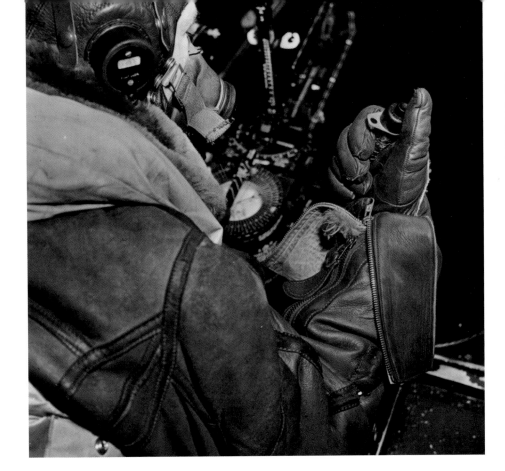

Left: A Lancaster bomb aimer on the job in his aircraft; below: The mid-section of the Avro Lancaster of the Battle of Britain Memorial Flight at RAF Coningsby, Lincolnshire. Opposite page: The pilot, right, and flight engineer of a Lancaster in the cockpit of the aircraft.

" 'Pilot to crew. The landing may be a bit difficult. You'd better bail out.'

"There was silence for a few seconds. Then Lanham called.

" 'What are you going to do, Jack?'

" 'I'm going to put her down at base. But I might make a balls of it.'

" 'You won't. This is your lucky night. I'm staying on board.'

"I warned them again, but nobody would go. We reached Wickenby five minutes later than the time on our flight plan, and the circuit was clear. I flew parallel with the runway, flashing dash—dot—dot—dot dot—dot—dash—dash—dash on the downward identification light. A green Very cartridge puffed up from the caravan. I made an accurate approach, but half a mile from touchdown I began to doubt the wisdom of my decision to land her. The way the wings were dipping, left to right and back to the left, was much worse than it seemed at 4,000 feet. However, there was a rythym in their rolling movement, and, picking the instant in mid-roll when the wings were level, I banged the main wheels down on the runway and held them there. *Baker Two* pulled up, squealing, in the last few feet of concrete. It was twenty-seven minutes past five.

"The muscles of my legs were tired from the unusual exercise of kicking *Baker Two*'s rudders for three hours, and it was some time before I could stand without support. The crew were less boisterous than usual, oddly gentle as they helped me to get into the crew bus, and had Walker taken to the sick bay. When we reached the briefing room, the Station Commander strolled towards me as I took a mug of cocoa from the padre's serving hatch.

" 'Not one of your better landings, Currie.'

" 'If I'd known you were watching I'd have tried harder.'

"He smiled and started to turn away, but Myring stopped him.

" 'The skipper was in difficulties, sir. He did bloody well to get it down at all.'

" 'Oh? What difficulties were you in, Currie?'

" 'I hadn't any aileron control, sir, and no flaps.'

" 'Why didn't you have aileron control?'

"Mentally I cursed Larry's intervention. I had hoped to report the incident in my own time to the debriefing officer, with a cigarette to smoke and my feet under the table, and let it go through the normal channels. Now here was the Station Commander staring at me imperiously, one eyebrow raised. The Squadron Commander was at his elbow, and other officers were edging closer. I hadn't had time to sip my cocoa.

" 'I'm afraid they broke off, sir.'

" 'Broke off. Are you serious, Currie?'

" 'Yes, sir. We got in a spin, in some cumulonimbus near the target.'

" 'I see.'

"He looked at me quizzically for a moment, then beckoned to the Squadron Commander and walked out to his car. I turned to the crew.

" 'I don't think he believed me.'

" 'He'll get a shock when he sees the kite, then.'

"That was the first of several inspections to be undergone by *Baker Two*, as expert and lay examiners looked at her damaged surface areas, sprung rivets and gaping wings. Meanwhile, I called at the sick bay to see the damaged Walker, who gave a pallid smile of recognition. The MO said he had concussion, confirming Myring's diagnosis, and that he would be moved to [a] hospital in a few hours' time. I trudged back to the hut.

"I felt slightly aggrieved when I was required to report to the Squadron

Commander a few hours later, while the rest of the crew slumbered on. Woody gave me a chair in his office and he sat at the desk making notes while I told him what had happened to *Baker Two*. When I had finished, he looked up with a smile.

" 'Well, I think it was a magnificent show. Has it shaken you up a bit?'

" 'No, I don't think so, sir. We're all fine, except for the engineer. He's gone into Rauceby.'

" 'Would you like to take a few days leave?'

"I considered the kindly suggestion. We had returned from our last leave on Friday night, and this was Tuesday. The state of our finances varied from poor to very poor. Even Fairbairn's fabulous wealth could be measured in terms of shillings, and I decided that more time off would only be an embarrassment.

" 'No, thank you, sir. I think we'd better get on with the tour.'

"His smile became a grin.

" 'Had enough leave for a while, hm?'

" 'That's right, sir.'

"I was pleasantly surprised by the reactions of my colleagues on the squadron, some humorous, all generous. It was good to realize that each could emerge from his own embattled world to remark and applaud another's fortune. But, putting personal thoughts aside, the raid had not been a success. Nature, more terrible and more effective than all man-made defences, had thrown her arms around the city and its ravaged streets and protected it from further horrors. Twenty-five of us had taken off from Wickenby; four thought that they had bombed the target, eight had bombed on ETA, not altogether certain where they were, six had been unable to reach Hamburg and had bombed some other town, three had jettisoned the bomb load in the sea, three had given up the sortie, and one did not return."

Left: Vickers Wellington bombers on a practice mission over central England; above: Allied aircraft bombing targets in Hamburg harbor.

Squadron Leader Jack Currie, second from left, served as a stretcher bearer and as an ambulance driver in London while awaiting his flying training which he received in the United States. In the RAF, he flew Lancaster bombers on the operational tour that he described in his excellent book *Lancaster Target*. Following that tour he was a Halifax bomber instructor before returning for a second tour of duty in Bomber Command in which he flew Mosquitos with the Pathfinder Force until the war in Europe ended. After the war he continued to serve as a pilot in the Royal Air Force until 1964.

ADOLF GALLAND

Many years ago I first met the German Air Force General Adolf Galland at a gathering in which a small, select group of high-achieving American, British, and German fighter pilots of the Second World War spoke about their flying careers and experiences. My initial impression of him that evening in a Virginia suburb of Washington, DC, was of a man who was relaxed and comfortable with his opinions and experiences, and seemingly quite open to conversation about them.

As personalities, most of the fighter pilots I have known were actually not very like the stereotype that frequently comes to mind about such aerial knights . . . ultra aggressive, narcissistic, cavalier, cool, calculating, focused, situationally aware, often a "chick magnet," boisterous, ostentatious, colorful,

fun-loving, free spirited . . . hunters.

While most (probably all) of these high achievers shared certain characteristics, as well as, perhaps, more than their share of luck in having survived their wartime experience, as personalities most of them have been pleasant, approachable, affable, and exceedingly generous with their time, memories, and perspectives.

One such was Adolf Galland, whom I came to know to some extent through our conversations and correspondence, and through some of his writing. We explored his military career in considerable detail and he always responded with interest and refreshing candor. Here is a rather wide-ranging assortment of his thoughts, responses, recollections, and remarks.

From the beginning of the Second World War, to the end of 1941, including the British retreat from Dunkirk, the Battle of Britain, and the initial German attack on the Soviet Union, General Adolf Galland was credited with more than seventy aerial victories. In the summer of 1941, at the age of twenty-nine, he was appointed General of the Fighter Arm of the German Air Force: "In the opening encounters of the Battle of Britain, the English were at a considerable disadvantage because of their close formation. In the Spanish Civil War we introduced a wide-open combat formation in which great intervals were kept between the smaller single formations and the groups, each of which flew at a different altitude. This gave us a number of important advantages: greater air coverage; relief for the individual pilot who could now concentrate more on the enemy than on keeping formation; freedom of initiative right down to the smallest unit without loss of collective strength; reduced vulnerability, as compared to close formation; and most

important of all, better vision. The first rule of all air combat is to see the opponent first. Like the hunter who stalks his prey and manoeuvres himself into the most favorable position for the kill, the fighter in the opening of a dogfight must detect the opponent as early as possible in order to attain a superior position for the attack.

"The British quickly realized the superiority of our combat formation and readjusted their own. At first they introduced the so-called 'Charlies': two flanking planes following in the rear of the main formation, flying slightly higher and further out, on a weaving course. Finally, they adopted our combat formation entirely. Since then, without any fundamental changes, it has been accepted throughout the world. Werner Mölders was greatly responsible for these developments.

"From the very beginning, the English had an extraordinary advantage which we never overcame throughout the war: radar and fighter control. For us and for our Command, this was a surprise and a very bitter one. The English possessed a closely knit radar network conforming to the highest technical standards of the day, which provided [RAF] Fighter Command with the most detailed data imaginable. Thus the British fighter was guided all the way from takeoff to his correct position for attack on the German formations. We had nothing of the kind. In the application of radio-location technique the enemy was far in advance of us. Under the serious threat for England arising from the German victory in France— no one described it more forcefully than Churchill in his memoirs—the British Command concentrated desperately on the development and perfection of radar. The success was outstanding. Our planes were already detected over the Pas de Calais while they were still assembling, and were

Among the greatest ace fighter pilots of the German Air Force in the Second World War was Adolf Galland, being assisted here by one of his ground crewmen.

never allowed to escape the radar eye. Each of our movements was projected almost faultlessly on the screens in the British fighter control centers, and as a result, Fighter Command was able to direct their forces to the most favorable position at the most propitious time. Of further outstanding advantage to the English was the fact that our attacks, especially those of the bombers, were, from sheer necessity, directed against the central concentration of the British defense. We were not in a position to seek out soft spots in the defense or to change our approach and to attack now from this direction, now from that, as the Allies did later in their air offensive against the Reich.

"For us there was only a frontal attack against the superbly organized defense of the British Isles, conducted with great determination. Added to this, the RAF was fighting over its own country. Pilots who had baled [sic] out could go into action again almost immediately, whereas ours were taken prisoner. Damaged English planes could sometimes still reach their base or make an emergency landing, while for us engine trouble or fuel shortage could mean the end.

"Morale too and the emotions played a great part. The desperate seriousness of the situation apparently aroused all the energies of this hardy and historically conscious people, whose arms in consequence were directed toward one goal: to repulse the German invaders at any price."

Galland: "In summer and autumn of 1940, I shot down twenty-one Spitfires, three Blenheims, and one Hurricane. The battle was tough but it never violated the unwritten laws of chivalry. We knew that our conflict with the enemy was a life-and-death struggle. We stuck with the rules of a fair fight, foremost being to spare the life of a

defenseless opponent. The German Air Sea Rescue people therefore picked up any RAF or American pilot they found floating in the Channel as well as the German airmen.

"To shoot at a pilot parachuting would have seemed to us an act of unspeakable barbarism. I remember the circumstances when Göring mentioned this subject during the Battle of Britain. Only Mölders was present when this conversation took place near the Reichsmarshall's train in France. Experience had proved, he told us, that especially with technically highly developed arms such as tanks and fighter aircraft, the men who controlled these machines were more important than the machines themselves. The aircraft which we shot down could easily be replaced by the English, but not the pilots. As in our own case it was very difficult, particularly as the war drew on. Successful fighter pilots who could survive this war would be valuable not only because of their experience and knowledge but also because of their rarity. Göring wanted to know if we had ever thought about this. 'Jawohl, Herr Reichsmarshall!' He looked me straight in the eyes and said 'What would [you] think of an order directing you to shoot down pilots who were baling [sic] out?' 'I should regard it as murder, Herr Reichsmarshall,' I told him, 'and I should do everything in my power to disobey such an order.' 'That is just the reply I had expected from you, Galland.' In World War I similar thoughts had cropped up, but were just as strongly rejected by the fighter pilots."

Galland: "On the third day of the campaign, May 12th 1940, I managed to score my first kill. It is true to say that the first kill can influence the whole career of a fighter pilot. Many to whom the first victory over the opponent has been long denied either by unfortunate circumstances, or by

Preparing a Heinkel He-111 bomber for an attack on a target city in England.

Below: Part of the Chain Home radar system of WWII England; right:: A Mk IX Spitfire at Duxford, England.

bad luck can suffer from frustration or develop complexes they may never rid themselves of again. I was lucky. My first kill was child's play. I took all this quite naturally, as a matter of course. There was nothing special about it. I had not felt any excitement and I was not even particularly elated by my success. That only came much later, when we had to deal with much tougher adversaries, when each relentless aerial combat was a question of 'you or me.' On that particular day I had something approaching a twinge of conscience. The congratulations of my superiors and my comrades left an odd taste in my mouth. An excellent weapon and luck had been on my side. To be successful, the best fighter pilot needs both."

Why did you paint Mickey Mouse on your plane? Galland: "I like Mickey Mouse."

On September 7, the fourth phase of the Battle of Britain began. Reichsmarshall Hermann Göring visited the Channel coast to give the order that would launch more than a thousand aircraft, horizontal bombers, Stukas, fighters, and destroyers, the largest air armada ever assembled, in the first major mission on London. It was the first of thirty-eight such large-scale raids on the British capital. The targets were the dock installations and oil storage facilities on the Thames. In the subsequent raids the total weight of bombs released in each attack averaged about 500 tons and was normally delivered by a bomber force of between fifty and eighty aircraft being escorted by one fighter wing. Galland: "The assembly of our bombers and fighters took place in the vicinity of our fighter bases over some landmark on the coast at a predetermined altitude and zero hour. It happened more than

Spitfire pilots at RAF Hawkinge in Kent during the Battle of Britain; right: German airmen in France.

once that the bombers arrived late. As a result, the fighters joined another bomber formation which had already met its fighter escort and thus flew doubly protected; while the belated formation had either to turn back or make an unescorted raid usually resulting in heavy losses. Radio or radar guidance for such an assembly was not available; even our intercom did not work most of the time. These difficulties increased with the deterioration of the weather in the autumn and finally assumed the proportions of a tragedy.

"All formations had to take the shortest route to London, because the escorting fighters had a reserve of only ten minutes' combat time. Large-scale decoy manoeuvres or circumnavigation of the British AA zone were therefore impossible. The antiaircraft barrage around London was of considerable strength and concentration and seriously hampered the target approach of the bombers. The balloon barrage over

and around the capital made low-level attacks and dive-bombing impossible. The bulk of the English fighters were sent up to encounter the German raiders just before they reached their target. I know of no instance in which they managed to prevent the bombers from reaching their target, but they inflicted heavy losses on them and the German escort fighters."

June 21, a warm and sunny day on the Channel coast. In two earlier encounters that day with enemy aircraft, Adolf Galland had downed two Bristol Blenheim bombers, bringing his total of credited kills to sixty-nine. The alarm sounded on his airfield at four in the afternoon and all the remaining operational fighters of his outfit, 1/JG-26, took off to meet and engage with the approaching force of RAF Spitfires. Galland was quickly able to bounce one of the enemy aircraft and down his seventieth victory. But his regular

wingman had been shot down earlier in the day and had not yet returned to their base. Galland was alone and no one had witnessed his kill. He chose to follow his latest victim down. Galland: "Something hard hit my head and arm. My aircraft was in bad shape. The wings were ripped by cannon fire. I was sitting half in the open. The right side of the fuselage had been shot away. Fuel tank and radiator were both leaking heavily. Instinctively I banked away to the north. Almost calmly I noticed that my heavily damaged ME still flew and responded tolerably well with the engine cut off. My luck has held once more. I was thinking, and I will try to glide home. My altitude was 18,000 feet.

"My arm and head were bleeding. But I didn't feel any pain. No time for that. Anyhow, nothing precious was hurt. A sharp detonation tore me out of my reverie. The tank, which up to then had been gurgling away quietly, suddenly exploded. The whole fuselage

was immediately aflame. Burning petrol ran into the cockpit. It was getting uncomfortably hot. Only one thought remained: *Get Out, Get Out, Get Out!* The cockpit roof release would not work—must be jammed! Shall I burn alive in here?—I tore my belt open. I tried to open the hinged top of the roof. The air pressure on it was too strong. Flames all around me. I must open it! I must not fry to death in here. Terror! Those were the most terrible seconds of my life. With a last effort I pushed my whole body against the roof. The flap opened and was torn away by the airstream. I had already pulled her nose up. The push against the joystick did not throw me entirely clear of the burning coffin, which a few minutes before was still my beloved and faithful ME-109. The parachute on which I had been sitting was caught on the fixed part of the cockpit roof. The entire plane was now in flames and was dashing down to earth with

me. With my arm around the aerial mast I tugged. I pushed against anything I could find with my feet. All in vain! Should I be doomed at the last moment although I was already half freed? I don't know how I got free in the end. Suddenly I was falling. I turned over several times in the air. Thank God. In my excitement I nearly operated the quick harness release instead of the cord. At the last moment I noticed that I was releasing the safety catch. Another shock! The parachute and I would have arrived separately. A jerk, and like a pendulum I was suspended from the open parachute. Slowly and softly I floated down to earth.

"Below me a column of black smoke marked the spot where my ME crashed. By rights I should have landed in the Forest of Boulogne like a monkey on a tree, but the parachute brushed a poplar and then folded up. I landed rather luckily in a soft, boggy meadow. Up to now I had been under

high tension of nerves and energy. I collapsed. I felt as wretched as a dog. Shot and bleeding profusely from head and arm, with a painfully twisted ankle which started to swell immediately, I could neither walk nor stand up. Suspicious and unfriendly French peasants came at last and carried me into a farmhouse. The first Germans I saw were men of the Todt Organization from a nearby building site. They packed me into a car and took me back to my base at Audembert."

Douglas Bader: "I saw pieces flying off my crate. The nose dipped. I looked round—the tail unit had practically gone . . . nothing else to be done but to get out as quickly as possible. That was easier said than done, especially as the plane dived vertically and began to spin. I pulled myself up with my hands. I had already got one leg outside. The other one, the right one, was wedged inside. I tugged and the plane tugged

Below: Luftwaffe Bf109 fighters; bottom: Adolf Galland; right: The B-17F *Sugar Puss* on its hardstand at the 384th Bomb Group base, Grafton Underwood.

too. Then I was shooting through the air minus my right leg. That was going down with the aircraft . . ."

In August of 1941, RAF Group Captain Douglas Bader, the famous fighter pilot who had lost his legs in a 1931 flying accident, was shot down in a dogfight over the Pas de Calais in German-occupied France. At his air base, Adolf Galland and his staff were surprised and pleased to find them-selves hosting the legendary English ace. They enjoyed his presence briefly before hustling him off to prison camp. In describing his departure from the badly damaged Spitfire in 1941, he referred, of course, to the prosthetic legs he had been fitted with in 1931. When he awoke in the Saint-Omer Hospital he asked about his artificial legs and was told that the right one was there by his bedside. He then asked that the wreckage of his plane be searched for his missing left artificial leg. The Germans made the search

and located the damaged missing leg in a field near the wreckage. General Galland had it repaired by one of his mechanics and soon Bader was practic-ing walking in the hospital ward.

As soon as Bader was well enough, Galland had him brought by staff car to the German's base where he was the "guest" of the JG-26 officers. While there, Galland and his men asked no military questions of the Englishman. They had been strictly forbidden from doing so. As Bader relaxed a bit in their company, Galland invited him on a tour of the base. Bader asked the general if he would have a message dropped over England to tell his wife that he was well and would she please have a package put together containing his spare pair of prosthetic legs, a spare uniform, a pipe, and some tobacco. In the base tour, Galland showed Bader his personal fighter plane and Bader asked if he might sit in it. Galland agreed and, when the Englishman was

B-17s of the 390th Bomb Group based at
Framlingham, their fighter escorts weaving
above them.

comfortably seated in the cockpit the general explained the fighter in considerable detail. Bader showed his interest and finally asked: "Will you do me a great favor?"

"With pleasure if it is in my power."

"At least once in my life I would like to fly a Messerschmitt. Let me do just one circle over the airfield," said Bader.

Looking him in the eyes, Galland said: "If I grant your wish, I'm afraid you'll escape and I should be forced to chase after you. Now [that] we have met we don't want to shoot at each other again, do we?" They both laughed and Bader was returned to the hospital.

Later that day, Galland called Reichsmarschall Göring and told him of Bader's request for the spare pair of legs, and Göring agreed that the request should be met and told Galland to contact the RAF on the international SOS wavelength and offer a safe conduct to a British plane which could land on an airfield near the French coast and unload the package for Bader. The radio contact was made; the request confirmed by the RAF. While preparations for the delivery were under way, Douglas Bader managed to tie some bedsheets together, lower himself from a window of the hospital, and escape, much to the concern and embarrassment of General Galland. Meanwhile, the RAF did visit the general's airfield, along with a few others in the area, dropping a number of bombs. Clearly, chivalry had lost what significance it may have had for the British with the incessant German bombing of London and other British cities. They did, however, also drop the large box containing the items that Bader had requested. The box displayed a large red cross and, in German, THIS BOX CONTAINS ARTIFICIAL LEGS FOR WING COMMANDER BADER, PRISONER OF WAR. In the aftermath,

The restored P-51D Mustang *Kimberly Kaye*
at Duxford, Cambridgeshire.

General Adolf Galland photographed at Duxford, England, during the filming of *Battle of Britain* in 1968.

Bader was soon recaptured and subsequently made several additional escape attempts, all abortive.

Late in 1944, as the fortunes of the Luftwaffe were declining, Göring's influence with Hitler was also in a tailspin. He had long since lost the marginal respect his pilots had for him. His incompetence as leader of the air force was blatantly evident. Little cliques of his officers quietly formed in clandestine bids for influence and position. Morale in the service was at an all-time low and when word of the unprecedented unrest got to the Reichsmarschall he summoned all of his top fighter and night-fighter leaders to a meeting in which his self-control vanished, replaced by a raging tirade of insults and abuse that roused in his audience a bitter, rebellious reaction.

Galland: "We fighter pilots were indeed prepared to fight and die, as we had proved often enough, but we were not prepared to let ourselves be insulted or blamed for the disastrous situation in the air over the Reich. Most unnecessarily Göring ordered on top of all this that his impossible speech should be recorded. The record was to be played at intervals to the pilots at action stations."

In January 1945, General of the Fighter Arm Adolf Galland was officially relieved of his command and sent on leave. With that followed a massive wave of unrest among the fighter pilots of the German Air Force. This led to further heated exchanges between Göring and some of the key Luftwaffe leaders. Eventually, Hitler learned about the situation in his air force and Galland was ordered to meet with him at the Reich's Chancellery. He then told Galland that he had ordered "a stop to all this nonsense." Next came an invitation from Göring for Galland to meet

with him at Carin Hall, his country home. There, he offered Galland the opportunity to form and lead a unit of the new ME-262 jet fighters. He was entitled to staff the unit with officers of his own choosing, and the officer chosen to replace him as General of the Fighter Arm would have no jurisdiction over Galland's unit—all of this on Hitler's orders.

Galland recalled the early morning of May 22, 1943, when he had met with Willy Messerschmitt at the planemaker's testing airfield near the Augsburg Messerschmitt facility. On the field, Galland noticed two examples of the new ME-262 jet fighter, two-engined, low-slung radical designs with swept wings and no propellers. He was invited to fly one of them after watching a brief demonstration flight by the chief test pilot. He sat in the cockpit and listened to instruction from the pilot. As the engines were started, one of them caught fire and Galland got out quickly. The fire was soon extinguished and he climbed into the second aircraft. These early model 262s had tail wheels, thus the nose blocked the pilot's forward view of the runway in the takeoff roll. At 120 mph the little fighter gently lifted off the runway.

Galland: "For the first time I was flying by jet propulsion! No engine vibrations. No torque and no lashing sound of the propeller. Accompanied by a whistling sound, my jet shot through the air. Later, when asked what it felt like, I said, 'It was as though angels were pushing.' On landing, I was more impressed and enthusiastic than I had ever been before. Feelings and impressions were no criteria, but the performance and characteristics were ascertained. This was not a step forward; this was a leap!"

With the end approaching for the

German Reich, Adolf Galland gathered his officers for a final meeting on April 25, 1945. He told them: "Militarily speaking the war is lost. Even our action here cannot change anything. I shall continue to fight, because operating with the ME-262 has got hold of me, and because I am proud to belong to the last fighter pilots of the German Luftwaffe. Only those who feel the same are to go on flying with me."

GEOFFREY PAGE

" 'Page! You're about to fly a Spitfire. But if you break your neck, don't blame me!"

"Half an hour later, I reported back to Squadron Leader Leigh. 'Happy about it, Page?'

" 'I think so, thank you, sir.' The CO. grunted and knocked his pipe out on the machined piston head that served as an ashtray. 'Let's have the takeoff drill again.'

" 'R-A-F-T-P. Radiator, airscrew, flaps, trim, and petrol.'

"I had been sitting in the cockpit of a Spitfire for half an hour memorizing the cockpit procedures for takeoff, flight, and landing. I was now back for my final examination before being let loose with a machine.

"The CO asked a few more questions; then, satisfied that at least I understood the theory, he stood up, and, with pipe firmly clenched between his teeth, beckoned me to follow him to the aircraft. He stood by while I stepped onto the port wing and into the small cockpit. An airman climbed onto the wing behind me to help me with my parachute and harness.

"Word spread swiftly that an unusual first solo on type was taking place and soon ground and aircrews were gathering to watch with morbid interest. As soon as I was properly strapped in, the squadron commander climbed onto the wing for a final word. 'Don't forget,' he said, 'taxi out quickly and turn her into the wind—do a quick check and then get off. If you don't, the glycol will boil and so will my blood. Good luck!'

"I responded with a nervous smile, closed the tiny door, and turned to face the mass of dials, buttons, and levers. For a moment panic seized me and the temptation to undo the straps and get out was very great—but it was quickly replaced by a strong desire to urinate!

"The enquiring voice of the airman standing by the starter battery reminded me of the engine starting procedure, and my nervous feeling passed with the need for concentrated action. Carefully, I recalled the squadron commander's words of instruction: throttle about half an inch open—gas on—nine full strokes in the KI—gas hand priming pump for a cold engine—propeller in fine pitch—brakes on—stick held back—press the starter button. I raised my thumb, the waiting airman replied with a similar sign, and I pressed the starter button firmly—the propeller began to rotate as the motor turned the twenty-four cylinders of the large Merlin engine.

"A trickle of sweat ran down my forehead. Suddenly the powerful engine coughed loudly, blew a short stream of purply-white smoke into a small cloud and roared into life. Remembering that I had little time to spare before the temperature reached the danger mark of 110°, I waved my hands across my face. The waiting airman quickly ducked under the wing and pulled away the restraining chocks. Glancing down, I was alarmed to see that the glycol coolant temperature had risen from zero to 70°. Releasing the brake, I eased the throttle open and the surge of power carried the aircraft forward rapidly over the grass.

"Was everything ready for a quick takeoff? I wondered. I figured I'd better call up Flying Control and get permission to scramble [take off immediately]. Pushing over the switch on the VHF box, I tried to transmit. 'Idiot!' I said to myself, 'switch the damn thing on.' Another glance at the temperature showed 95° and still a long way to go before turning into the wind. The radio came to life with a whine, and contact was made with a fellow human being. The controller's voice was soothing and for the first time since strapping me into the narrow cockpit, I relaxed slightly. But I was still none too happy.

"The temperature now read 105° and there were still a few yards to go, plus the final check. Softly I prayed for help.

"Temperature 107°.

"Now for the drill: R-A-F-T-P. R—the radiator—God alone knows how many times I'd vainly tried to open it beyond its normal point to try to keep the temperature down. A—airscrew in the fine pitch—that's okay. F—flaps.

"Temperature 109°. . .

"I abandoned the remainder of the cockpit drill and, opening the throttle firmly, started the takeoff, run. The initial kick from the rapid acceleration drove the worry of the engine temperature away for a while. Working the rudder hard with both feet to keep the sensitive little machine straight, I was too busy for other thoughts. Easing the stick forward, I was startled by the rapidity with which she responded to the elevator controls. The long nose in front of me obscured the rapidly approaching end of the airport, but by looking out at an angle I was able to get an idea of how far away it was. If the glycol boiled now at this critical stage, the aircraft would be enveloped in a cloud of white smoke that would prevent me from seeing the ground when the inevitable engine seizure and crash landing followed. Looking back into the cockpit again, I saw the hated instrument leering at me.

"110°.

"Accompanying the feeling of fear was a new sound. The wheels had stopped drumming and a whistling noise filled the air. The Spitfire soared gracefully into the air, thankful, as I was, to be away from her earthly bonds.

"Inside the cockpit, I worked des-

Right: Chalky vapor trails over the southern English town of Lewes mark the progress of RAF dogfights with invading Luftwaffe raiders in the Battle of Britain; below: A stained glass memorial window honoring the RAF ground control plotters of 1940; far right: The tool kit of an RAF ground crew mechanic who helped maintain Hawker Hurricane fighters at the Tangmere fighter station in Sussex.

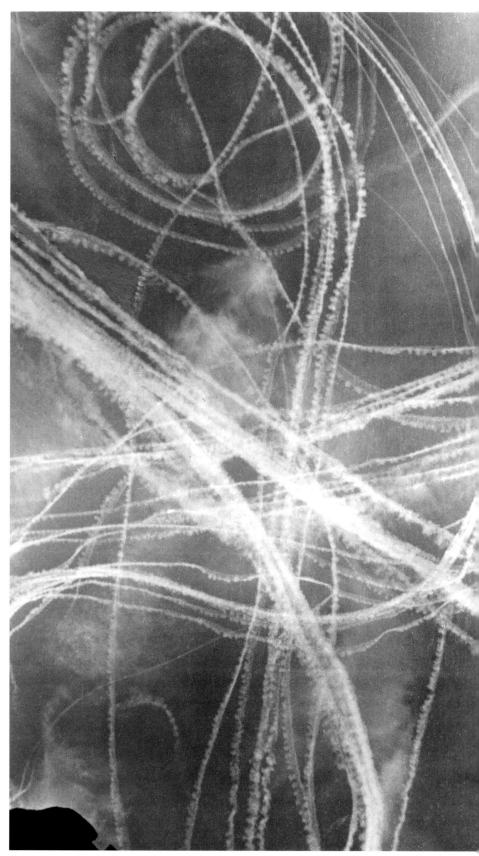

perately to get the undercarriage raised. The CO had explained to me that because the starboard aircraft leg hung down in front of the radiator when the wheels were lowered, this affects the cooling effect by the air-stream. By raising the wheels the air would pass unhindered through the radiator to do its work. But here I fell into trouble again. To raise the wheels, I had to move the selector lever, and this was on the right hand of the seat. I then had to pump them up with twenty movements by a long handle, also on the right. To do all this while flying the very sensitive aircraft meant using my left hand for the control column, while the right hand struggled with the undercarriage mechanism.

"The Spitfire was now about twenty feet up, gaining speed rapidly and skimming over the trees and hedges. I selected 'wheels up' and gave the handle a first stroke. The engine cut out for an instant and the nose plunged earthwards. Being unused to the technique of keeping my left hand absolutely still while the right one moved forward, I had inadvertently pushed the control column forward simultaneously with the first pumping stroke, thus causing the machine to dip suddenly. The negative gee placed on the carburettor had caused a temporary fuel stoppage. Some trees flashed by alongside the aircraft as a frightened pilot hauled back on the stick, and soon I was soaring skyward again, pumping frantically after removing my left hand from the control column. At this stage it was obvious that the Spitfire could handle herself better than I could. After this nightmare, the green light finally shone on the instrument panel, indicating that the wheels were in the locked-up position, and the engine temperature gauge showed a healthy fall. I took a moment to utter another silent prayer, this time of thanks.

"Now I had some breathing space, so I was able to look about and concentrate on the other aspects of flying the aeroplane. Throttling back the engine and placing the propeller in coarse pitch, I allowed myself the luxury of relaxing slightly and looked down on the beauties of the Norfolk Broads. However, the pleasures of the English countryside didn't last long. Glancing down and behind me, I was horrified to discover that the airport was nowhere in sight. The swiftness of the Spitfire had soon taken me out of sight of the landing ground, and although homing facilities were available over the R/T, pride stopped me from calling the flying control tower for assistance. Instead, a worried young man flew about the sky in circles anxiously peering down for a sign of home. Ten minutes later, relief flooded through me when the unmistakeable outlines of Norwich Cathedral appeared out of the summer haze, and from there the airport was easy to find. A minute later, the graceful plane was banking round the circuit preparatory to landing.

"Again I recalled the cockpit procedure given to me by the squadron commander: R-U-P-F—radiator, undercarriage, pitch, and flaps. This time the pumping down of the wheels came quite simply, and the other essential procedures prior to the final touchdown followed. The exhausts crackled delightfully as the engine was throttled back and the plane came in gliding fast over the boundary hedge. In the cockpit, I eased the stick back and the long streamlined nose rose up and cut out the forward view of the landing run. Looking out to the left, I carefully judged the height as the Spitfire floated gracefully a foot or two above the green grass, then losing speed she settled down on the ground to the steady rumble of the wheels. As soon as the machine had come to a halt, I raised the flaps and thankfully undid the tight-fitting oxygen mask. The pool of sweat that had collected trickled down my neck. With a newly born confidence, I taxied the machine back towards the waving airman near the hangar. Just as I removed my helmet and undid the confining harness and parachute straps, Dizzy Allen walked up.

" 'Back in one piece, I see. How'd you get on?'

"Trying to appear nonchalant, I replied, 'Loved every minute of it. She certainly handles beautifully.' The feeling of achievement obliterated the memory of the fear I'd felt during most of the flight, and now I felt justified in taking a place among my fellow fighter pilots."

Little Willie was the name painted just below the left canopy rail of the Hawker Hurricane of RAF Pilot-Officer Alan Geoffrey Page. Before the outbreak of World War II, Page had joined the University Air Squadron of London University, and completed his training at Cranwell. He was flying as a member of No 56 Squadron from Rochford on August 12, 1940, at the height of the Battle of Britain. He vividly recalled the events of that day: "One moment the sky between me and the thirty Dornier 215s was clear; the next it was crisscrossed with streams of white tracer from cannon shells converging on our Hurricanes.

"The first bang came as a shock. For an instant, I couldn't believe I'd been hit. Two more bangs followed in quick succession, and as if by magic a gaping hole suddenly appeared in my starboard wing.

"Surprise quickly changed to fear, and as the instinct of self-preservation began to take over, the gas tank behind the engine blew up, and my cockpit became an inferno. Fear became blind terror, then agonized horror as the

The ruin of the Tangmere control tower in the 1990s.

Below: The pilots of RAF Fighter Command were sometimes referred to as the Brylcreem Boys; right: The control column of a downed Vickers-Supermarine Spitfire fighter.

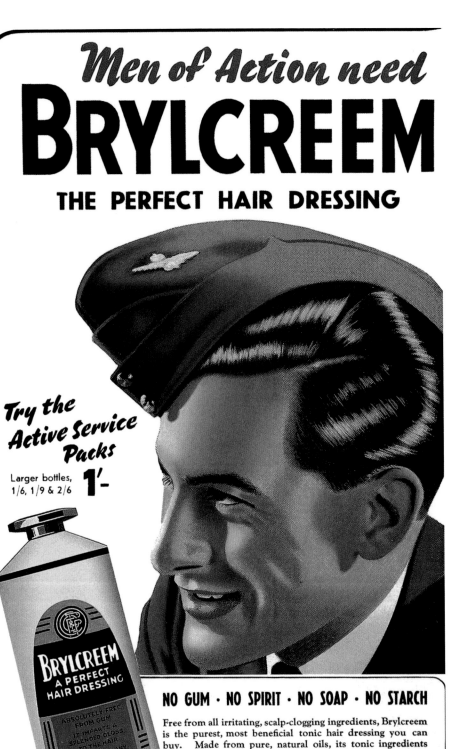

Men of Action need
BRYLCREEM
THE PERFECT HAIR DRESSING

Try the Active Service Packs

Larger bottles, 1/6, 1/9 & 2/6 **1'-**

BRYLCREEM
A PERFECT
HAIR DRESSING

ABSOLUTELY FREE
FROM GUM
IT IMPARTS A
SPLENDID GLOSS
TO THE HAIR
IT FIXES IT IN ANY
DESIRED POSITION

NO GUM · NO SPIRIT · NO SOAP · NO STARCH

Free from all irritating, scalp-clogging ingredients, Brylcreem is the purest, most beneficial tonic hair dressing you can buy.   Made from pure, natural oils, its tonic ingredients encourage healthy growth, remove all loose dandruff.

bare skin of my hands gripping the throttle and control column shriveled up like burnt parchment under the intensity of the blast-furnace temperature. Screaming at the top of my voice, I threw my head back to keep it away from the searing flames. Instinctively, the tortured right hand groped for the release pin securing the restraining Sutton harness.

" 'Dear God, save me . . . save me, Dear God,' I cried imploringly. Then as suddenly as terror had overtaken me, it vanished with the knowledge that death was no longer to be feared. My fingers kept up their blind and bloody groping. Some large, mechanical, dark object disappeared between my legs and cool, relieving fresh air suddenly flowed across my burning face. I tumbled, sky, sea, sky, over and over as a clearing brain issued instructions to outflung limbs. 'Pull the rip cord—right hand to the rip cord.' Watering eyes focused on an arm flung out in space with some strange meaty object attached at the end.

"More tumbling—more sky and sea, but with a blue-clad arm forming a focal point in the foreground. 'Pull the rip cord, hand' the brain again commanded. Slowly but obediently the elbow bent and the hand came across the body to rest on the chromium ring but bounced away quickly with the agony of contact.

"More tumbling, but at a slower rate now. The weight of the head was beginning to tell. Realizing that pain or no pain, the rip cord had to be pulled, the brain overcame the reaction of the raw nerve endings and forced the mutilated fingers to grasp the ring and pull firmly.

"It acted immediately. With a jerk the silken canopy billowed in the clear summer sky. Quickly, I looked up to see if the dreaded flames had done their work, and it was with relief that

I saw that the shining material was unburned. Another fear rapidly followed. I heard the murmur of fading engines and firing guns, but it was the sun glinting on two pairs of wings that struck a chill through my heart. Stories of pilots being machine-gunned as they parachuted down came flashing through my mind, and again I prayed for salvation. The two fighters straightened out and revealed themselves to be Hurricanes before turning away to continue the chase.

"It was then that I noticed the smell. The odor of my burnt flesh was so loathsome that I wanted to vomit. But there was too much to attend to even for that small luxury.

"Self-preservation was my first concern, and my chance for it looked slim. The coastline at Margate was just discernible six to ten miles away; 10,000 feet below me lay the deserted sea. Not a ship or a seagull crossed its blank, grey surface.

"Still looking down, I began to laugh. The force of the exploding gas tank had blown every vestige of clothing off from my thighs downwards, including one shoe. Carefully I eased off the remaining shoe with the toes of the other foot and watched the tumbling footwear in the hope of seeing it strike the water far beneath. Now came the bad time.

"The shock of my violent injuries was starting to take hold, and this, combined with the cold air brought on a shivering attack that was quite uncomfortable. With that, the parachute began to sway, setting up a violent oscillating movement with my torso acting as a human pendulum. Besides its swinging movement it began a gentle turn, and shortly afterwards the friendly shoreline disappeared behind my back. This brought with it an *idée fixe* that, if survival were to be achieved, then the coast must be kept

in sight. A combination of agonized curses and bleeding hands pulling on the shrouds finally brought about the desired effect, and I settled back to the pleasures of closing eyes and burnt flesh.

"Looking down again I was surprised to find that the water had come up to meet me very rapidly since last I had taken stock of the situation. This called for some fairly swift action if the parachute were to be discarded a second or two before entering the water. The procedure itself was quite simple. Lying over my stomach was a small metal release box that clasped the four ends of the parachute harness after they had passed down over the shoulders and up from the groin. On this box was a circular metal disc that had to be turned through ninety degrees, banged, and presto! The occupant was released from the 'chute. All of this was extremely simple except in the case of fingers that refused to turn the little disc.

"The struggle was still in progress when I plunged feet first into the water. Despite the beauties of the summer and the wealth of warm days that had occurred, the sea felt icy cold to my badly shocked body. Kicking madly, I came to the surface to find my arms entangled with the multiple shrouds holding me in an octopus-like grip. The battle with the metal disc still had to be won, or else the waterlogged parachute would eventually drag me down to a watery grave. Spluttering with mouthfuls of salt water, I struggled grimly with the vital release mechanism. Pieces of flesh flaked off and blood poured from the raw tissues.

"Desperation, egged on by near panic, forced the decision, and with a sob of relief I found that the disc had surrendered the battle. Kicking away blindly at the tentacles that still entwined arms and legs, I fought free and swam fiercely away from the nightmare surroundings of the parachute. Wild fear died away and the simple rules of procedure for continued existence exerted themselves again. 'Get rid of the 'chute, and then inflate your Mae West, and float about until rescued.

" 'That's all very well,' I thought, 'but unless I get near to the coast under my own steam, there's not much chance of being picked up.' With that, I trod water and extricated the long rubber tube with which to blow up the jacket. Unscrewing the valves between my teeth, I searched my panting lungs for extra air. The only result after several minutes of exertion was a feeling of dizziness and a string of bubbles from the bottom of the jacket. The fire had burnt a large hole through the rubber bladder.

"Dismay was soon replaced by fatalism. There was the distant shore, unseen but positioned by reference to

the sun, and only one method of getting there, so it appeared. Turning on my stomach, I set out at a measured stroke. Ten minutes of acute misery passed by as the salt dried about my face injuries, and the contracting strap of the flying helmet cut into the raw surface of my chin. Buckle and leather had welded into one solid mass, preventing removal of the headgear.

"Dumb despair then suddenly gave way to shining hope. The brandy flask, of course. This was it—the emergency for which it was kept. But the problem of undoing the tunic remained, not to mention that the tight-fitting Mae West covered the pocket as another formidable barrier. Hope and joy were running too high to be deterred by such mundane problems, and so, turning with my face to the sky, I set about the task of getting slightly tipsy on neat brandy. Inch by inch my ultrasensitive fingers worked their way under the Mae West towards the breast pock-

et. Every movement brought with it indescribable agony, but the goal was too great to allow for weakness. At last the restraining copper button was reached—a deep breath to cope with the pain—and it was undone. Automatically my legs kept up their propulsive efforts while my hand had a rest from its labours. Then, gingerly, the flask was eased out of its home and brought to the surface of the water. Pain became conqueror for a while and the flask was transferred to a position between my wrists. Placing the screw stopper between my teeth, I undid it with a series of head-twists and finally the great moment arrived— the life-warming liquid was waiting to be drunk. Raising it to my mouth, I pursed my lips to drink. The flask slipped from between my wet wrists and disappeared from sight. Genuine tears of rage followed this newest form of torture, which in turn gave place to a furious determination to swim to

safety.

"After the first few angry strokes, despair returned in full force, ably assisted by growing fatigue, cold, and pain. Time went by unregistered. Was it minutes, hours, or days since my flaming Hurricane disappeared between my legs? Was it getting dark or were my eyes closing up? How could I steer towards the shore if I couldn't see the sun? How could I see the sun if that rising pall of smoke obscured it from sight?

"That rising pall of smoke . . . that rising pall of smoke. No, it couldn't be. I yelled, I splashed the water with my arms and legs until the pain brought me to a sobbing halt. Yes, the smoke was coming from a funnel—but supposing it passed without seeing me? Agony of mind was greater than agony of body and the shouting and splashing recommenced. Looking again, almost expecting that smoke and funnel had been a hallucination, I gave a fervent gasp of thanks to see that, whatever ship it was, I hove to.

"All of the problems were fast disappearing and only one remained. It was one of keeping afloat for just another minute or two before all energy failed. Then I heard it—the unmistakable chug-chug of a small motorboat growing steadily louder. Soon it came into sight with a small bow pouring away to each side. In it sat two men in the strange garb of the British Merchant Service. The high-revving note of the engine died to a steady throb as the man astride the engine throttled back. Slowly the boat circled without attempting to pick me up. A rough voice carried over the intervening water. 'What are you? A Jerry or one of ours?'

"My weak reply was gagged by a mouthful of water. The other man tried as the boat came full circle for the second time. 'Are you a Jerry, mate?'

"Anger flooded through me. Anger, not at these sailors who had every reason to let a German pilot drown, but anger at the steady chain of events since the explosion that had reduced my tortured mind and body to its present state of near-collapse. And anger brought with it temporary energy. 'You stupid pair of fucking bastards, pull me out!'

"The boat altered course and drew alongside. Strong arms leaned down and dragged my limp body over the side and into the bottom of the boat. 'The minute you swore, mate,' one of them explained, 'we knew you was an RAF officer.'

"The sodden dripping bundle was deposited on a wooden seat athwart ships. A voice mumbled from an almost lifeless body as the charred helmet was removed. One of the sailors leaned down to catch the words. 'What did you say, chum?' 'Take me to the side. I want to be sick.'

The other man answered in a friendly voice, 'You do it in the bottom of the boat and we'll clean it up afterwards.'

"But habit died hard and pride wouldn't permit it, so, keeping my head down between my knees, I was able to control the sensation of nausea. Allowing me a moment or two to feel better, the first sailor produced a large clamp knife. 'Better get this wet stuff off you, mate. You don't want to catch your death of cold.'

"The absurdity of death from a chill struck me as funny and I chuckled for the first time in a long while. To prove the sailor's point, the teeth chattering recommenced. Without further ado, the man with the knife set to work and deftly removed pieces of my life jacket and tunic with the skill of a surgeon. Then my naked body was wrapped up in a blanket produced from the seat locker.

"One of them went forward to the engine and seconds later the little boat was churning her way back to the mother ship. The other sailor sat down beside me in silence, anxious to help but not knowing what to do next. I sensed the kindness of his attitude and felt that it was up to me to somehow offer him a lead. The feeling of sickness was still there from the revolting smell of burnt flesh, but I managed to gulp out, 'Been a lovely . . . summer, hasn't it?' "

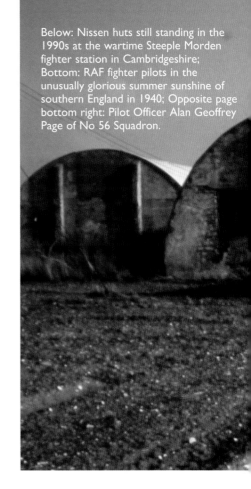

Below: Nissen huts still standing in the 1990s at the wartime Steeple Morden fighter station in Cambridgeshire; Bottom: RAF fighter pilots in the unusually glorious summer sunshine of southern England in 1940; Opposite page bottom right: Pilot Officer Alan Geoffrey Page of No 56 Squadron.

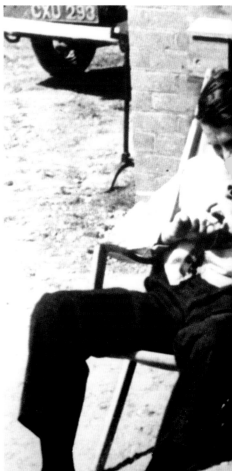

RAF Group Captain Peter Townsend of No 85 Squadron, Tangmere.

PETER TOWNSEND

Pilot Hermann Wilms, Unteroffizier Karl Missy, and the crew of a Heinkel He-111 bomber of 2nd Gruppe, KG 26, the Lion Geschwader, were not operating from their permanent field at Westerland on February 2, 1940. They had been sent to Schleswig, north of Hamburg, for their next mission, and takeoff was set for dawn the following day. The crew of the Heinkel was made up of Wilms, Missy, a gunner, Peter Leushake, and an observer, and flight mechanic Johann Meyer, all unteroffiziere.

The sounds of a snowplow and a hundred soldiers busily clearing three feet of snow from the runway awoke them at two that morning. The Wilms crewmen went out to help with the clearing. When that job was done, the crew of the Heinkel went to briefing. They were told to take off in three-minute intervals and head west. They were to expect to sight an Allied convoy steaming south, off the northeast coast of England. They were to attack it and shadow the convoy, reporting its position.

Early that same morning, Flight Lieutenant Peter Townsend and the pilots of "B" Flight, No 43 Squadron RAF, dozed fitfully in the cold discomfort of their dispersal hut at Acklington in Northumberland. When awakened, they were sent to their Hurricane fighters which were parked on the far side of the field. A fierce wind blew across the airfield and they arrived to find that some of the aircraft starter batteries had gone flat, requiring some of the planes to be cranked by hand. That procedure could scrape the skin from one's knuckles and even break a wrist through propeller kickback; even

decapitation was a possibility should one slip forward into a propeller. The superb Rolls-Royce Merlin engines were started and the B Flight pilots taxied the Hurricanes back over to their dispersal area where the duty corporal then reported to the sector headquarters: "Blue and Green Sections, B Flight, 43 Squadron at readiness.

"Just after nine a.m., the Danby Beacon radar station duty officer noted blips on his screen which indicated unidentified aircraft approximately sixty miles out and approaching the English coast at an altitude of 1,000 feet. He passed the plots immediately to Fighter Command which relayed them to 13 Group and to the Acklington Sector station which telephoned 43 Squadron dispersal. An order was issued scrambling Blue Section to Angels One (1,000 feet).

"Jim Hallowes and Tiger Folkes flanked Peter Townsend in the climb out and [the] turn to 180° at full throttle. Hallowes flew on Townsend's left; Folkes on his right. As they searched the cloud base, the large, dark shape of a Heinkel bomber appeared, slightly above and to their right. The Hurricanes banked into a climbing right turn and Townsend's thumb move[d] onto the gun button on the spade grip of his control column."

"Achtung, Jaeger," yelled Peter Leushake, the observer in the Heinkel, warning his fellow crewmen of the approaching Hurricanes. In firing range, Townsend pressed the gun button. His bullets killed Leushake instantly; Johann Meyer lay mortally wounded by bullets to his stomach. Now Townsend and Folkes were closing on the bomber and overtaking it as they all entered the cloud cover, dangerously close to one another. Folkes fighter and the Heinkel emerged together, the bomber trailing black smoke and turning towards the shoreline.

The gunner, Karl Missy, had been badly wounded in the back and legs, but was somehow able to keep firing his machine gun as Wilms, the pilot, struggled to control the damaged bomber. He managed to maintain enough height to barely clear the cliff tops near Whitby and several housetops there. The sight of the low-flying disabled enemy plane terrified a young girl as it appeared to pass her house at eye level. Police Special Constable Arthur Barratt recalled when the stricken German plane passed low overhead "with three of our fighters round him like flies round a honey pot." He estimated that the plane would come down near Sneaton Castle and roared off in his patrol car toward it.

Crumpled in his swivel seat and suffering considerable pain, Karl Missy continued to operate his gun as Wilms guided the bomber to what he hoped would be a safe touchdown on the snow-covered surface ahead. His mind was consumed with thoughts and fears about what it would be like to be a prisoner of war in the hands of the English enemy. He was suddenly jarred back into reality as the big Heinkel lurched and slammed down through a line of telegraph poles and their wires before floating on toward a barn beyond them. Wilms made one final attempt to haul the bomber back into the air and over the barn, but it was hopeless and the Heinkel slithered over the fresh snowpack.

Two hundred feet above this scene, Townsend's Hurricane circled and watched the snow and mud trailing in the wake of the enemy plane as it plunged on into a tree line, shedding its right wing and violently ripping around to come to rest only a few yards from the edges of Bannial Flat Farm where Constable Barratt and a small gathering of farmhands stood.

They all rushed up onto the wing of the plane, the first enemy aircraft to fall on British soil since 1918. As they neared the cockpit they saw Wilms trying to burn the aircraft's papers. Two of his crew were leaning against him and groaning.

The German pilot climbed from the wreck as Barratt and the others brought the rest of the crew members out. Now a little group of local onlookers was gathering around the downed bomber and Wilms raised his hands and shouted at them, "Boom!, Boom!" causing them to back away. A small fire erupted in the wreck and the farmhands used fire extinguishers and threw shovelfuls of snow on it.

RAF intelligence officers soon arrived to retrieve some of the German papers that had survived Wilms' effort to burn them. A Mrs Smales called to Karl Missy, urging him to come out of the aircraft, but his legs were shattered. He used his arms to lower himself down to where Johann Meyer lay screaming with the agony of his stomach wound. Missy tried to help the man, but only collapsed himself with blood now pouring freely from his own wounds. He yelled to Wilms, "Hermann, come and help Johann." He then managed to drag himself from the plane. Wilms dragged the body of Leushake out from the shattered Perspex of the nose and then went back to drag Meyer out.

Missy and Meyer were carried into Mrs Smales' house where she made tea for them, gave them hot water bottles, and wrapped them in blankets. They were also given cigarettes. Shortly, a local doctor arrived and injected Meyer with morphine. He cut off Missy's boots and put his legs in splints. Missy's left leg had been broken; his right leg mutilated. An ambulance appeared and took Meyer

and Missy to the hospital. There Meyer died of his wounds. Later that evening, Karl Missy's right leg was amputated; his other leg put into a plaster cast.

In the hospital, communication was difficult. Karl Missy spoke no English; his head nurse spoke no German. Still, her care gave the German airman hope. In his continuing pain and worry, he received a visitor the next day—Peter Townsend, the man who had shot him down. Townsend: "Sister Oldfield met me in the corridor and told me that Missy was very ill and that they didn't know whether he would pull through, so I should only stay two minutes. Then she opened the door of Missy's ward and I entered, walking straight up to his bed. I held out my hand and, turning towards me, he clasped it with both of his until it hurt. But it was the way he looked at me that I can never forget. We had no common tongue, so could only communicate as the animals do, by touch, by expression, and by invisible means. As he took my hand Missy had in his eyes the look of a dying animal. If he had died I would have been his killer. He said nothing and only looked at me with a pitiful, frightened, and infinitely sad expression in which I thought I could recognize a glimmer of human gratitude. Indeed, Missy felt no bitterness. He sank back on the pillows and I held out the bag of oranges and the tin of fifty Players I had brought for him. They seemed poor compensation. Then I left Karl Missy and went back to Acklington and the war.

"I called on Karl Missy one day in the summer of 1968, in the tidy little house where he was born and where his father had started him off in the plumbing trade. The old man had brought Karl up to be honest

RAF Group Captain Peter Townsend with his rigger and fitter at Tangmere in 1940.

and hardworking like himself, and a first-class tradesman. It was from this house, where I now sat talking to Karl Missy, that he had set out on the road which would lead him into a gun battle with me.

"He reminded me of what I had said (his pilot, Wilms, had interpreted) when I saw him in Whitby hospital the next day. 'Sorry for having shot you down. English and German airmen should only try to compete with each other in peacetime.' Looking at him now and listening to his story, I realized how futile it was to have tried to kill a man like Missy—a good, solid type, the kind the world needs. It was a pity that he had to leave his plumbing and go off to fight for Adolf Hitler. But now that affair is settled; Karl Missy and I can look each other straight in the face, despite the harm I have done to him. That is a small victory for humanity."

"The greater issues were beyond us. We sat in a tiny cockpit, throttle lever in one hand, stick in the other. At the end of our right thumb was the firing button, and in each wing were four guns. We aimed through an optical gun sight, a red bead in the middle of a red ring. Our one concern was to boot out the enemy."
—Group Captain Peter Townsend

"By the rules of war it was justifiable to kill a pilot who could fight again. But few of us could bring ourselves to shoot a helpless man in cold blood."
—Group Captain Peter Townsend

"We were not, thank God, involved in the intimate, personal killing of men which is the lot of the infantry—though we fired with the same bloody end in view. The men inside the aircraft must be killed, or maimed, or taken prisoner, otherwise they would return to battle. Very few of us thought of it that way, and this gave to our battle in the air the character of a terribly dangerous sport and not of a dismal, sordid slaughter."
—Group Captain Peter Townsend

" 'Don't you ever cry, don't ever shed a tear. / Don't you ever cry after I'm gone.' There seemed nothing melancholy in those lilting words and the catchy little tune seemed suited to our mood. Some of us would die within the next few days. That was inevitable. But you did not believe it would be you. Death was always present, and we knew it for what it was. If we had to die we would be alone, smashed to pieces, burnt alive, or drowned. Some strange protecting veil kept the nightmare thought from our minds, as it did the loss of our friends. Their disappearance struck us as less a solid blow than a dark shadow which chilled our hearts and passed on. We seemed already to be living in another world, separate and exalted, where the gulf between life and death had closed and was no longer forbidding."
—Group Captain Peter Townsend

"I stuck my toothbrush in my left breast pocket, took my sponge bag, and made for the bathroom. The Duke of Kent, brother of the King, was expected at 10 a.m. Halfway to the bathroom, the alarm went. 'No 85 Squadron, scramble!' A few minutes later I was climbing away from Croydon at the head of six Hurricanes. 'One hundred plus' from Fliegerkorps II were heading for Dover. By the time we arrived they were on their way home. Sergeant Sam Allard, our finest pilot, sent a stray ME-109 into the sea. Back at Croydon, Tim Maloney—adjutant of 85, its friend, father and managing

director—told me to hurry. The Duke was waiting. 'Get the pilots lined up. He wants to meet them' Tim told me. 'Flight Lieutenant Hamilton from Canada,' I introduced Hammy, who to my consternation seemed to be squinting at me and doing his best not to laugh. I retreated a pace and glanced down the front of my tunic. On my left breast, beside my wings and a solitary DFC ribbon, a gleaming white toothbrush stuck out of my pocket. I had taken it into battle with me. The Duke refrained from comment."
—Group Captain Peter Townsend

The He-111 bomber shot down by Peter Townsend on February 2, 1940.

DUKE WARREN

Identical twin boys were born to Marie and Earl Warren of Nanton, Alberta, Canada, on May 28, 1922. Douglas and Bruce grew up in the farming community of Wetaskiwin, halfway between Edmonton and Red Deer. There they became interested in flying and read all they could on aviation in the magazines of the time, especially *Aeroplane* and *Flight*. In early September 1939, the Warrens moved to another farm, at Ponoka near the Battle River, and with the outbreak of the Second World War, Canada declared war on Germany and the Warren boys both decided to join the air force.

As they were not yet eighteen, they had to wait until the following May to enlist. Their parents were distressed by the boys' decision; their father was an unswerving isolationist: "Let them fight amongst themselves; don't send our men to be killed over there. We shouldn't be sending our young men overseas. Let the Europeans fight their own wars." But his sons were determined and, after passing their medical examinations, were sworn in to His Majesty's Royal Canadian Air Force; given their service numbers, train tickets, and instructions to report to No. 2 Manning Pool, Brandon, for six weeks of preliminary training. After Brandon, they were sent to Mossbank, Saskatchewan, and there they were given their first flights, brief rides in an obsolete Fairey Battle. Next, they were posted to Initial Training School at Regina where they were taught the theory of flight, as well as courses in navigation, radio, engines, mathematics, science, Morse code, and had the experience of a Link trainer.

The twins enjoyed their stint at the ITS and wrote frequently to their parents of their activities and adventures. "We felt that by writing often and assuring them that we were happy and in good health it would lessen their anxiety."

During their time at Regina, the boys' pay was very low and they were usually short of cash. Bruce Warren augmented his income by pressing clothes for his fellow trainees, for which he received ten cents for a pair of trousers and twenty-five cents for a tunic. The better-off trainees were getting additional funds from the families or from previous employers who helped them by making up the difference between the service pay and what they had earned as civilians.

In those days, RCAF aircrew selection was made at the Initial Training Schools. Most of the trainees wanted to be pilots, but other aircrew positions were needed too; wireless operators, air gunners, observers, flight engineers, navigators, and bomb aimers. The selection depended heavily on the largely subjective opinions of the training staff, as well as examination results, and the current needs of the training schools. As much as possible though, they did try to accommodate the wishes of the trainees. To their immense satisfaction, both Douglas and Bruce were selected for pilot training and sent to No 5 Elementary Flying Training School at High River, Alberta. Douglas: "Now we were allowed to wear the coveted 'white flash' in our service caps, indicating that we were under training for aircrew duties in the RCAF. We were promoted to the rank of Leading Aircraftman or LAC and our daily pay was increased to $1.50 plus 75 cents flying pay. We were rich!

"We were to receive fifty hours flying time in forty-nine days. I began flying at High River with my assigned instructor, a small American from Los Angeles named Dusenbury who got a surprise when he learned that he was to instruct Warren, B. and Warren, D. He just couldn't tell us apart and he was never able to tell us apart all the time we were at High River.

"For most of our young lives we had both had this overpowering desire to fly. Now we were on the way and were terribly enthusiastic about the thrill of flying, actually learning to handle the controls, and becoming confident that we would qualify as pilots.

"At High River, the routine was half the day at ground school and the other half flying. The Tiger Moth was one of the basic training aircraft of the British Commonwealth Air Training Plan. The Moth had a top speed of 110 mph and the RCAF had an inventory of more than 1,500 of them. The field is located in an area of strong winds which, often at ground level or a few hundred feet up, would exceed the stalling speed of the Tiger Moth. Sometimes an aircraft would appear in the circuit and, when flying directly into the wind, would stay in one spot relative to the ground if the pilot adjusted the power to give an airspeed equal to the windspeed.

"In summer, another problem was severe turbulence encountered as a result of surface heating at midday. Consequently, flying was scheduled in the early morning and was sometimes shut down for a few hours during the most turbulent time of the day. Sudden thunderstorms or hail were also a menace—the latter particularly so, for the Tiger Moth wings and part of the fuselage were fabric covered and hailstones could do a lot of damage. If a hailstorm was thought to be likely, all aircraft on the ground were pushed into the hangar.

A restored Mk 1a Spitfire over southern
England in 2008.

Below: The pilot's view from the cockpit of a Mk 1 Spitfire; right: A flown postal cover commemorating the first flight of the Spitfire prototype.

Those in the air would stay away until the storm passed, or divert to another base. The decision to divert would have to be made by the pilot, as there were no radios fitted to the Tiger Moths. Indeed, there was no electrical communication between student and instructor. Gosport tubes had been fitted. This was a simple system developed at Gosport Aerodrome, England, in World War I. It consisted of tubes—rather like a garden hose—between the cockpits and stethoscope-like fittings plugged into it. There were earpieces on one's head so that the student could hear the instructor's shouts. Most of the conversation was instructor to student, and only infrequently student to instructor.

"Parachutes were carried on all flights, and we students were told they cost $450 each and that if we carelessly damaged one we would be charged.

"Dusenbury tried to keep all his students at about the same level, and at the end of the week of 27th July my twin and I had each flown about seven and a half hours and our instructor was satisfied with our progress. We knew that if the weather remained good we would most likely be sent solo the following week. Being sent solo is a high point in every pilot's life and the occasion is never forgotten."

At the end of August the Warrens' training at High River was finished. Bruce had logged a total flying time of 60.55 hours; Douglas a total of 57.45 hours. They were then posted to No 34 Service Training Flying School at Medicine Hat and as they approached the start of flying training there, they were thrilled to learn that they were to be taught to fly the North American Harvard. Those who were trained on the Harvard generally went on to fly fighters, which was the

dream of the Warrens, even though it meant yet another new ground school course. The Harvard was an excellent advanced trainer with a top speed of 212 mph and was a handful for most trainees. It was said that, if you could fly a Harvard you could fly anything.

"We were assigned to Flying Officer Cherrington, a taciturn RAF officer who was bitter about being selected to instruct in Canada rather than remaining in the UK on operations. He seemed to discourage any conversation other than the strictly necessary. When Cherrington realized that we were twins, and identical twins looking very much alike, there was some discussion as to whether we should be 'split up' and one of us sent to another instructor. In the end we were both kept as students of Cherrington and, as it was customary to use only the last name, he called my twin Warren Mark I and I was Warren Mark II.

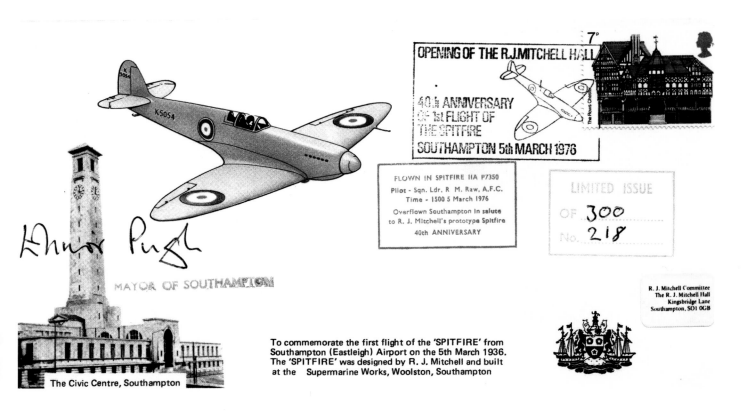

MAYOR OF SOUTHAMPTON

The Civic Centre, Southampton

OPENING OF THE R.J.MITCHELL HALL

40th ANNIVERSARY OF 1st FLIGHT OF THE SPITFIRE

SOUTHAMPTON 5th MARCH 1976

FLOWN IN SPITFIRE IIA P7350
Pilot - Sqn. Ldr. R M. Raw, A.F.C.
Time - 1500 5 March 1976
Overflown Southampton in salute to R. J. Mitchell's prototype Spitfire
40th ANNIVERSARY

LIMITED ISSUE
OF 300
No. 218

R. J. Mitchell Committee
The R. J. Mitchell Hall
Kingsbridge Lane
Southampton, SO1 0GB

To commemorate the first flight of the 'SPITFIRE' from Southampton (Eastleigh) Airport on the 5th March 1936. The 'SPITFIRE' was designed by R. J. Mitchell and built at the Supermarine Works, Woolston, Southampton

"It was quite a big step to go from the relatively light Tiger Moth to the Harvard, which weighed three times as much, with about four times the horsepower and twice the speed. The cockpit was big and roomy compared with the Moth, and a decided change was having the instructor behind you rather than in front. The center of gravity in the Moth was such that if flown solo, it was flown from the back seat. To get the students used to this, we always flew in the back cockpit, dual or solo.

"Our new instructor had a habit which we found most annoying. Later on, when we ourselves were experienced and took an instructors' course, we discovered that it was a dangerous habit as well. At times, if Cherrington became impatient with what the student was doing, he would grab the control column and thrash it about, hitting one's knees. Since the importance of transferring control of the aircraft by the words 'You have control' and the response 'I have control' had been drilled into us, when Cherrington did this we were never sure who had control at the moment. Sometimes control would be transferred in the normal manner, but other days it was seldom done in the approved way. Much later, when overseas, we met one of the RAF officers who had instructed at Medicine Hat. When we brought up the subject of Cherrington and his habits, we were told that not only was he bitter about the task of instructing, but he also was suffering from a severe stomach ulcer. This made us feel sorry for him, but he had caused us some worrisome moments.

"On 16th December, after a check ride with the Flight Commander, we were put up for our wings test with the Chief Flying Instructor. We qualified for our pilot's wings, and on the evening of the 18th there was a party in the airmen's mess. Our instructor, Flying Officer Cherrington, approached us during the evening and told us we had both received an above-average mark on our wings test. He congratulated us and then said: 'I have a question: why do you both have the same nickname?' This went back to our school days when we had a teacher who explained to the class that we were duplicates of each other. The other youngsters began calling us 'Dupes' and, not caring for this rather unflattering nickname, we changed it to Duke, and it stuck. Bruce was Duke Mark I and Douglas was Duke Mark II.

"On 19th December, our Wings Parade was held. Coupled with the joy of graduating as pilots, there was some 'bad news.'" Of the thirty-seven graduates in their class, Bruce stood eighth and Douglas ninth. The first eight students were granted commissions, so Bruce became Pilot Officer Warren

and Douglas became Sergeant Warren. "We were ordered to report to Halifax on January 5, 1942, for embarkation and decided to see what could be done to reverse the decision, which would cause us to be split up. We went to RCAF Headquarters at Calgary and, not knowing the administrative organization, asked to see the padre. The gist of our argument was that our academic marks and the results of our flying tests were remarkably close, and that the arbitrary 'cutoff' would not have resulted in this problem had we not been twins. Furthermore, we argued, if it was not possible to rectify the situation by granting me a commission, we would be satisfied if the RCAF would cancel my brother's appointment and make him a sergeant. The padre listened intently and was sympathetic. He told us that there was an army regulation that allowed an older brother to 'claim' a younger brother,

and asked us who was the older. We had never really thought about it, but my brother quickly said he was the older, and if necessary would claim me. This meant that we would have to be together and would not be divided by his commission. The padre made several phone calls and we then were granted a series of interviews, the final one being with a group-captain who assured us that our case would be looked at closely and, if our air and ground marks were as close as we stated, very sympathetic consideration would be given to commissioning me. But nothing could be done until our records arrived and by then we would probably by on our way to Halifax. We left feeling confident.

"From our first awareness of the world around us, there always existed an 'us and them' feeling . . . the special feeling that identical twins have for each other. My twin was always of paramount importance in my life, and

others were secondary. I know that he felt the same.

"We arrived at Halifax and here started the physical separation of my brother and me, for he was allocated a room in the officers' quarters and I in the NCO quarters. On 8th January we marched to the ship and in a few hours were bound for England."

The Warrens were sent to Bournemouth, a resort town on the south coast where, as arriving aircrew from overseas, they were to be held until assigned to an Advanced Flying Unit (AFU) or an Operational Training Unit (OTU). There they had a lot of free time and spent much of it together. "We enjoyed Bournemouth but we were impatient to 'get on with the job.' In mid-February, some postings came in for men who had arrived about the same time we had. My commission had not yet been decided, but we were told that the details of our training had been forwarded to

The main runway at RAF Tangmere, West Sussex, in the 1990s; far left: The North American Aviation logo of the company that built the P-51 Mustang long-range escort fighter.

A German Air Force Heinkel He-111 bomber heading for a target in England during the Blitz of 1940.

Ottawa and that it looked favorable for us. Bruce and I discussed what our best course of action would be if we were split up. We knew that it was not likely that we would be on the same draft for further training at an Advanced Flying Unit or Operational Training Unit. There the training was on higher performance aircraft and one also became familiar with flying conditions in England. The often cloudy weather, frequent fog, and the numerous railways going in all directions could easily confuse a young pilot for the first few hours.

"We decided to make no effort to go to the same AFU, but would, of course, be happy if we were sent together. However, when we finished our OTU, we would see what squadrons we were sent to, and then decide 'who was the oldest' and which of us would 'claim' his younger brother. My brother was sent to No 8 AFU at Hullavington in Wiltshire, and

I to a unit at Hastings, Sussex. Then, about three weeks after I arrived in Hastings, a message came through that I had been granted a commission dated from December 19, 1941. This gave me the same seniority as Bruce. I was ordered to report back to Bournemouth. Time went slowly as I waited for a posting to an AFU. I was concerned that my brother would get so far ahead of me in training that we might be separated for that reason. This was really the first time in our lives that we had been apart for more than a few days. I missed him and frequently thought of him, but not in a manner which would be called 'worrying about him.' I was always confident that he was okay and I know he felt the same about me.

"Eventually, I was posted to No 17 AFU at Watton, Norfolk, where, having not flown for nearly four months, I was given one and a half hours instruction on a Miles Master

Mk II and sent solo. I enjoyed flying at Watton AFU, a necessary step before going on to an Operational Training Unit where I would be flying either Hurricanes or Spitfires. In the meantime, I was learning about flying in English conditions—reduced visibility, instrument flying, and map reading, which often presented problems with so much detail and so many railway tracks, as compared with flying in Alberta. I left Watton having flown a little over seventeen hours in the Master aircraft. My posting was to 57 OTU, a Spitfire outfit at Hawarden, Cheshire. I was very pleased with my good fortune. In April, my twin had been posted to No 52 OTU, also a Spitfire unit, at Aston Down, Gloucestershire. Our luck held. We were both training to be operational on the same type of aircraft.

"Toward the middle of June, Duke (we both called each other Duke) phoned to say how pleased he was

with the squadron he had been posted to, No 165 RAF at Heathfield, near Ayr in Scotland. He said that his flight commander, Squadron Leader Archie Winskill, had promised to try to arrange with Fighter Command personnel that I be posted there.

"The course finished and my posting came in, to No 403 (RCAF) at Digby in Lincolnshire. I left for my new squadron with mixed feelings, glad to be going operational but sorry it was not north to Scotland. My new Squadron commander at Digby was Squadron-Leader Al Deere, a renowned Battle of Britain pilot who had baled [sic] out so many times he was nicknamed 'the man with nine lives.' A New Zealander who had joined the RAF, he was an exceptional leader and was highly respected by all the fighter pilots in England. He was rather a quiet man, whose sense of humor showed through a small smile. I liked him immediately. But my stay at

Digby was very short. In two days, a message arrived changing my posting from 403 Squadron to 165 RAF at Heathfield. Squadron Leader Winskill had carried through his promise to try to get me sent to his squadron and, of course, I was delighted. I had not mentioned my desire to join 165 Squadron to Squadron Leader Deere, but when I happened to meet him just before my departure I explained why I was so pleased about the change. He said very little, but seemed quite understanding, and wished me luck.

"On my arrival at Heathfield I was sent to the officers' quarters where I was shown Duke's room and I stowed my kit. Duke knew I was coming, but no exact time had been given; nor was it possible to do so with train travel the way it was then. For that reason he was carrying on a normal day of duty, and was down on the flight line. It was a great thrill for both of us when I arrived at 'A' Flight to join him there, for this was the culmination of all our hopes of the past eighteen months, to be on a fighter station together and, equally important, here we were, physically together again, a wonderful feeling which is hard to understand if you are not a twin.

"I was interviewed by Squadron Leader Winskill and expressed my gratitude for what he had done for us. I liked him at once, and not just because he had brought us together. He was the sort of officer everyone liked—a very handsome man, who we later found often had calls from the Windmill girls (of the famous London theatre). He never took himself too seriously and was an excellent leader. He told me that he was placing me in 'A' Flight along with Duke, and was confident that we would be a credit to the squadron.

"After a short time on the squadron, and after I had been assessed in the air, Duke and I became a more or less permanent section of two. This was the smallest fighting section of a squadron; a flight might be four aircraft, two sections of two, or sometimes six, three sections of two. Generally, the squadron put up twelve aircraft, in three flights . . . red, yellow, and blue. Often it happened we flew as Yellow Three and Four. Duke was considered the more experienced since he had arrived first on the squadron, so he flew as Yellow Three and I as Four.

"In August there were rumors of a move south to 11 Group, Fighter Command, which covered the southeast portion of England. This was the area where most fighter operations took place at this time, and corresponded roughly to the area where the Battle of Britain had been fought two years before. In effect, we were going into battle. One night Duke and I had a serious talk about the future and what it might bring. We knew casualties occurred among fighter pilots everywhere, but were far more likely to happen in the south where air-to-air fighting took place. We recognized that one or both of us might be injured in a crash, wounded, or killed, and reading the intelligence reports we recognized this was more than likely, or at least a 50-50 chance. We were not distressed by our conversation. Our main concern was the likely reaction of our parents. We were well aware of our parents' strong reaction against our joining up because of the potential danger. Even before leaving Canada we had witnessed the reaction of parents and families who had lost a member due to a flying accident or some other tragic event. We had a Christian belief that everything was in the hands of

Douglas Bader, left, and James "Ginger" Lacey visiting a set of the *Battle of Britain* film.

the Lord, and He would make the decisions. We agreed on one thing, and cautioned each other not to 'go crazy' if one of us should see the other shot down or crash . . . and go against impossible odds in a fit of rage. Looking back now, perhaps we were being overconfident in our ability to maintain self-control under those circumstances, but luckily, we were never put to the test. Soon we flew south to Eastchurch to become part of 11 Group, Fighter Command, and the famous Biggin Hill wing.

"165 was considered a 'new squadron' in that it had not operated in the south before, and further training was thought to be needed. We did two training flights and a sweep toward Le Touquet on 17th and 18th August. Pilots taking part in the combined Dieppe operation on the 19th knew it was a 'big show.' Only later did we learn how big it was. The RAF had flown almost 3,000 sorties, the Luftwaffe 945. At the time, it was thought losses were about equal, 100 aircraft on each side, but it was later found that the Germans had only lost fifty, whereas the Allies lost 106.

Shortly after Dieppe, the squadron left Eastchurch and relocated to Gravesend, where the officers were quartered in a beautiful old English home, Cobham Hall. Just prior to coming south, our CO, Squadron Leader Winskill, was posted and his replacement was Squadron Leader Jim Hallowes, an older man who had been a prewar Sergeant Pilot and was a 'Halton Brat' (a person who had joined the RAF as a boy apprentice and been sent to Halton for technical training). Squadron Leader Hallowes had distinguished himself flying at Dunkirk and in the Battle of Britain. He was rather more reserved than Squadron Leader Winskill, but was respected by everyone and we had

great confidence in him as our leader.

"The squadron took part in many sweeps over France. Sometimes we escorted bombers, Blenheims, Venturas, or Bostons.

"Whenever possible, we went up to London. The train service was frequent and took about forty-five minutes to 'the Big Smoke,' as it was called by some then. We went to museums, shows, and cinemas. We didn't drink and seldom went to pubs unless we were with other pilots on some special occasion.

"Fighter Command had a policy of rotating squadrons through its various stations, and in early November, 165 was moved down to Tangmere, near Chichester, on the south coast. We were sorry to leave Gravesend with its proximity to London, and the friends we had made there, but Tangmere was a much better location for the winter, for it had permanent runways. It was also a famous fighter station that had played a prominent part in the Battle of Britain. At Tangmere, we trained in night flying and during the period fom mid-November 1942 to mid-February 1943, I flew sixteen night sorties and twenty-three operations, while Duke flew twelve night sorties and twenty ops. Most of these night sorties were in cooperation with searchlight practice. The searchlights would try to illuminate the aircraft as if they were enemy aircraft. When caught by a searchlight I would lower my seat, turn the cockpit lights as bright as I could, and fly instruments till the exercise was over."

For the Warrens at Tangmere, a combination of night and day flying continued until the last week of March, when the squadron was moved north again, this time to Peterhead near Aberdeen. "On a training flight, a new Aussie pilot

collided with Duke and chopped off part of his tail. Both pilots landed safely, the Aussie's aircraft with a much shorter prop. When he brought his parachute into the crew room, Duke was ready to really tear a strip off the Aussie. But the Aussie never came into the crew room. He was so embarrassed, ashamed, and sorry for what he had done, he wouldn't leave his aircraft. It ended with Duke going out to tell him 'Don't worry. It could happen to anyone.'"

No 165 Squadron was moved again as the year advanced, to Exeter and then to Kenley, another famous Battle of Britain station and part of the Biggin Hill wing. Prior to this move, in August, Bruce Warren was assigned to, and completed, the Fighter Leaders' course for prospective Flight Commanders, at RAF Charmy Down near Bath in Somerset.

"Duke and I roomed together in the old prewar officers' mess, which was luxurious in comparison with other quarters we had been in. We had a nice room, and the ablutions were just down the hall. This gave rise to a funny situation which, at first, we didn't know about. A few days after the squadron arrived at Kenley, the station commander, a Group Captain, came to the flight to meet the pilots. He was introduced and said how pleased he was to meet us, for he thought the squadron had a lunatic pilot. Each morning, he would be in the washroom shaving, when a Canadian officer would come in, say 'Good Morning, sir,' wash, and leave. He couldn't understand what was going on with this chap. The reason this was our morning drill was that we had only one electric razor between us, which we shared. Whoever shaved first went and washed up while the other one shaved and then washed up. Since the Group Captain didn't realize there was a set of identical twins on the squadron, to him it was just a crazy pilot.

In mid-September, No 165 moved again, this time to RAF Church Stanton near Taunton, Somerset. "Finally, our fervent wishes and prayers were answered. For sixteen months we had suffered under the Fw 190s while flying Spitfire Vs. Now we were issued Spitfire IXs and what a wonderful change! The Mk IX maximum speed was 416 mph at 27,500 feet. It had a ceiling of 45,000 feet and a vastly superior rate of climb. At 22,000 feet and above, we had the edge on any German fighter at the time. One of the good things about the new aircraft was that all of the instruments and controls were exactly the same as on the Spit V, so it was easy to feel at home in the cockpit. The big difference was the power, rate of climb, and the ceiling. We were often at 40,000 feet and with no pressurization and no heat. So we were issued submariners' big wool sweaters and socks. Later we received electric bootees to keep our feet warm, but we found them prone to short circuits and burning if they were worn very long. When this happened, the pilot had to struggle in the cockpit to pull the heating plug out."

In January 1944, after eighteen months of operational flying, the Warren twins were sent on a rest leave. At that point in the war, RCAF aircrew in England were given the option of taking leave in Canada, but many declined the opportunity for a month at home for various reasons, not least the long, unpleasant sea journey. The Warrens chose not to return home because of the emotional trauma their mother and father had experienced when they had left for the war. They knew how upset their parents would be when the time

came for them to return to England and decided not to tell their parents about their leave.

Once again the boys were posted, to No 58 OTU at Grangemouth in Scotland, and Bruce left for their new station. Prior to the move, Douglas was sent to the Fighter Leaders' course at Aston Down. When he arrived at Grangemouth, Douglas was immediately moved to a satellite field called Balado Bridge, where he lived in a cold and miserable Nissen hut in the Scottish winter. "The hut we lived in had a small potbellied coal stove which would have been okay except the coal was so poor in quality that to get it to burn we used to bring back a partly used oxygen bottle from the flight line, and with a bit of wood and paper and the oxygen, we could get a good, basic fire going."

The twins were shuffled around some more as 1944 wore on, doing a stint in bomber affiliation work. In July, they were posted to No 66 Squadron, which was part of 132 Royal Norwegian Wing RAF. In August, the squadron moved across the Channel to airfield B16 in France. "The Battle of Falaise stretched over several days as the Canadian and British armies fought down the road from Trun to Chambois. American forces were met on 21st August and the gap was closed. At this time, our aircraft were armed with two 20mm cannon and two .5 Browning machine guns. They could be fired independently or all together. It was an armament that we especially liked because the pilot had an option as to what to use on various targets. Furthermore, if we did not carry drop tanks, we could put a 500-pound bomb under the fuselage and a 250-pound bomb under each wing.

"All accounts of the battle give great credit to the work of the

WAAFs on a motorbike at RAF Tangmere in the summer of 1940.

THE STORY OF THE PLANE THAT BUSTED THE BLITZ!

SPITFIRE

fighter-bombers. Among these, the Typhoons played the major role. They were armed with four 20mm cannon[s], bombs, and rockets, and were especially effective against the German tanks. We Spitfire pilots ensured air superiority as well as doing armed recce and fighter-bomber attacks. Losses were heavy, both in the Typhoon squadrons and the Spitfire squadrons doing fighter-bomber work. By their nature, low-level attacks are dangerous, and when a plane is hit low down there is very little time to bale [sic] out.

"We attacked horse-drawn transport along with staff cars and trucks. The German soldiers would hold the horses' bridles as the horses reared in fright and pain. Duke and I, having grown up on a farm with an intimate knowledge of horses, felt especially sorry for the animals because they could not understand what was happening to them.

"B16 was located near a small village, Villons les Buissons, and was what we called a 'tar paper strip.' This was a method of laying down a heavy, black, treated paper in an attempt to control the dust during takeoff and landing. The dust was very damaging to the motors . . . Typhoons especially, because of the sleeve valves in the 24-cylinder Napier engines. They experienced more engine failures, as the Merlin could eat dust better than the Sabre engine.

"Operations continued. The Germans had left pockets of men in Le Havre, Calais, Boulogne, Ostend, and other places. Now the Canadian army was fighting to get them out. We continued to support them with low-level attacks and bombing. We seldom saw a German fighter, as they were being held back to intercept bombers or defend against the British army. What we were doing was dangerous, for all these places had lots of antiaircraft guns, and the gunners had been practicing with live targets since 1940 and were accurate. So we lost pilots all the while. One of the puzzles we thought about for some time was why pilots didn't bale [sic] out when they lost a wing. This was a fairly common occurrence. If the wing was hit by flak it would be seriously weakened and break off when the G-forces built up in the pullout. The aircraft appeared to fall quite slowly, with seemingly gentle rotation. Following a number of these incidents, the medical officers found that when the wing broke off, the initial rotation was so fast it flung the pilot's head sideways and broke his neck.

"On my forty-fourth operational sortie I almost 'bought it.' The squadron had been detailed to bomb heavy artillery sites at Calais. We approached at about 15,000 feet and I trimmed for the dive. Then there was a loud explosion under the aircraft and sunlight came through a hole in the left side of the cockpit. An 88mm flak gun had exploded a shell just under my left wing. A piece passing through drove the trim wheel into my leg, carried on up, bending my parachute D ring as it passed, and ended up in a small tin box in my upper left breast pocket. One might ask why a fighter pilot would be flying with a small tin box in his pocket. This was a special box used as part of an escape kit. If a person was shot down and trying to evade and hide from the enemy, it was difficult to get safe drinking water. In the small box was a large rubber balloon which you filled with water from a ditch or dirty pond. You popped in a tablet, shook it up well and, in fifteen minutes you could drink it. It tasted like water from a ditch, but all the bugs in it were killed. The fragment of shell had pierced the tin box deeply, but had the box not been there, it would have pierced my body and perhaps my heart.

"Since I had been trimmed for the dive in level flight at normal speed, the aircraft was difficult, but not impossible, to control. Duke realized I had been hit, but he could tell I still had control, and so proceeded with the attack while I returned to base. I could

smell something burning, but was not aware of where it was coming from, which was rather a worry. After landing I found the red-hot fragment had ignited the kapok in my Mae West [life jacket] and it was smouldering. I kept the fragment, D ring and tin box for souvenirs.

"In late fall, Paul Gibbs, who commanded B Flight, finished his tour, and I took over as his replacement. This was a great occasion for Duke and me, now both flight commanders in the same squadron. Every senior officer we spoke to said that they had never known such a situation before. Further, the fact that we were Canadians and identical twins at that level in the Royal Air Force was quite unique. It really went smoothly, for we had roomed with Paul Gibbs so we knew all the ins and outs of B Flight as well as A Flight. There were many in the squadron who didn't even try to tell us apart, because there was really no need. We were recognized by our rank and position and the pilots followed the orders that came down. One thing was not so good. We often flew separately with a small section, so that cut down our operations together. However, on a squadron show we would both be flying."

On December 22, 1944, the Wing moved to Woensdrecht, in the Netherlands. "The Germans had been pushed back, increasing the range of London for their V-weapons. Now most of these were targeted at Antwerp. We were now on the main flight path of the pilotless aircraft. The pulse jet made a Br-r-r-r noise as it went along, till the timer cut the motor and deflected the elevators. The weapon then dived steeply and exploded when it hit the ground. As long as the Br-r-r-r was heard, it could be ignored, but if the noise suddenly cut out, most people took shelter.

All prudent people did. V-1s could be shot down by aircraft, and they were, both on the Continent and in the UK. The V-2 was a rocket and could only be destroyed by an aircraft if caught on the firing stand before launch. Some people, both service and civilian, found the V-1 attacks very trying, and some suffered nervous breakdowns. One of the more serious of these was a Norwegian military policeman who suddenly began shooting at anything that moved, including pilots on the ground."

In mid-December a signal arrived awarding the Distinguished Flying Cross to both Douglas and Bruce Warren. The citation read: "Flight Lieutenant Douglas Warren: Flight Lieutenant Warren during two tours of operational duties has shown outstanding skill and courage. His determination to engage and destroy the enemy in the air and on the ground is worthy of high praise. He has completed numerous missions on heavily defended ground targets and enemy shipping. He has participated in the destruction by cannon fire of twenty enemy vehicles and the explosion of the magazine of a large enemy strong point. By accurate bombing he has destroyed one enemy aircraft and shared in the destruction of another. On another occasion his accurate bombing severed an important rail link in Germany." "Flight Lieutenant Bruce Warren: This officer has led his flight with such skill and determination in attacks on ground targets that more than twenty vehicles have been damaged and many probably destroyed. During his numerous sorties he has destroyed two enemy fighters and participated in the destruction of a hostile bomber. His fine fighting spirit and zeal have set an excellent example to all."

In mid-February their commanding officer told the Warrens that he was trying to find replacements for them as they were nearly tour-expired, and that both Nos 127 and 66 Squadrons were being sent to a practice gunnery camp at Fairwood Common in Wales. While there, Bruce and Douglas were taken off the squadron. On February 13, both Warrens flew their final operational flights.

On February 27, a farewell party for the two Dukes was given in the officers' mess. A great concession was made by the mess in allowing their squadron NCOs to attend. This was seldom done, and the twins were honored by the way it was carried out. The Warrens regretted leaving the squadron, a close bond having developed among the men who had shared a common danger and had depended on each other for survival.

"A message arrived telling us that we were to attend an investiture at Buckingham Palace on 20th March. The reason we were selected to attend at the Palace was because we were doing nothing but waiting to go home. Men awarded the DFC and still flying operationally on a squadron were not sent to London for an investiture. Most often the award was presented at squadron level by a senior RAF officer. On the day of the investiture, when our turn came, Duke received his DFC from the King, and marched off. When I appeared before him, looking the same, and with the same surname, the King looked rather bewildered and said: 'I don't think I have ever done anything like this before,' meaning awarding similar decorations to a pair of twins.

"On 14th April, we boarded the USS *Mount Vernon*, a converted passenger liner, for the trip home. The *Mount Vernon* arrived at Newport News, Virginia, on the 23rd, and on

the night of the 25th we got on a train in Montreal for the trip west and our return home after three and a half years overseas. We arrived in Ponoka on Sunday the 28th, and went to our parents' farm. They were thrilled to see us, and our mother seemed quite hysterical. We knew it had been a terrible strain on them while we had been on operations overseas. They told us how especially worried they had been at the time of Dieppe when it was reported that some 100 Allied planes had been lost, and how relieved they were when they got mail from us after the battle.

"Duke became engaged to Lois Burroughs, a beautiful and charming girl we had gone to school with. Duke had had an understanding with her while we were overseas. On 11th June they were married. I was best man and had invited a special person for me, Melba Bennett from Edmonton, who would later become my wife."

The Warrens were determined to remain in the Royal Canadian Air Force and obtain permanent commissions. They steadfastly refused to take release from the service when ordered to do so. They were threatened with appointment as flying instructors, which in fact happened. Their new careers as instructors continued, along with a sprinkling of 'odd jobs' and assignments until, in October 1946, their persistence paid off and they were both granted commissions in the RCAF Permanent Force. They retained their rank and seniority.

In the immediate postwar years, Douglas's role in the Air Force included a posting as Chief Flying Instructor at the Sabre OTU at RCAF Chatham. Bruce left the service to become a test pilot with Avro in the early days of the CF-100 program. On April 5, 1951, he was killed in the crash of the

A Messerschmitt Bf109 fighter belly-landed on the coast of France in 1940.

second prototype.

Of the Warren twins, Hugh A. S. Johnson, who had been their squadron commander in both No 165 and 66 Squadrons wrote in his book, *Tattered Battlements*: "They were of the same height to an eighth of an inch, the same weight to a couple of pounds, always dressed alike and, though different in characters, were as similar physically as two peas in a pod. Everything they did they did together, and everything they had they shared, even their bank balance was common to both. As pilots they had the right mixture of determination, discretion, and dash to be successful and formidable. On the ground, while not overburdened with academic learning—indeed they often made heavy weather in the pronunciation of unfamiliar words—they both had vigorous, inquiring minds and little patience with tradition-bound methods or ways of thought. They had remained together throughout their careers in the service and liked to say that if only one of them had joined up, they could have worked alternate weeks. They were typical of their trade in never taking exercise, but unusual in that they neither smoked nor drank; photography was their main preoccupation and delight. They represented the new world at its best. And each, with an impartiality and detachment which was sometimes puzzling, called the other 'Duke.'"

The pilot and navigator of a Heinkel He-111 bomber in an attack of an English target city.

JOHN GODFREY / DON GENTILE

In the Second World War, American fighter pilots Don Gentile and John Godfrey flew together, as leader and wingman respectively, with the Fourth Fighter Group of the Eighth U.S. Army Air Force. They were based at Debden airfield near Cambridge, England, and by the end of their tours of duty they had jointly accounted for fifty-eight enemy aircraft destroyed. Of those victories, Major Godfrey was credited with eighteen aerial kills and twelve aircraft destroyed on the ground.

Johnny Godfrey learned to fly with the Royal Canadian Air Force. In Elementary Flying Training at Windsor, Quebec, his first instructional flight—and his first time in an airplane—was with a flying instructor with a perfect name for that profession, Hop Good.

After only seven hours of dual instruction, Good declared Johnny ready to solo. Like most beginning fliers, the young man came to grips with the reality of his situation as he taxied out for takeoff. The notion of self-preservation passed quickly as he focused on the task at hand and was reminded of the old line, "Just fly by the book and all will go well." He did and it did.

As his flight training progressed, he met and became best of friends with two more Americans who had come to Canada to take part in the war that the United States had not yet entered. Joseph Jack ("JJ") and Bobby Richards, both from New York. Together with Godfrey, they would join the rest of the 244 Americans who would volunteer to fly and fight for the the RAF and the RCAF in what were called the

Left: Major John Godfrey and, above, Major Don Gentile, both of the Fourth Fighter Group based at Debden in Essex.

The cockpit of an unrestored WWII P-51 Mustang fighter.

Eagle Squadrons. They were furtively recruited by an organization in New York City called the Clayton Knight Committee, whose role was to assist the American recruits to get flight training with the RCAF in Canada before being shipped to England for action with one of the three Eagle Squadrons. In fact, the recruits were violating strict U.S. neutrality laws at the time and might have been subject to serious penalities, including, but not limited to, the loss of their U.S. citizenship if charged and convicted. One former Eagle, James A. Gray (No 71 Eagle Squadron) recalled: "It was a curious situation. I didn't have to register for the draft . . . so I didn't have a draft notice. I wasn't trying to avoid the draft, which a number of the chaps were. I had been flying out of Oakland, California, airport where I soloed, and then went to the University of California where I joined the Civil Pilot Training Program and got myself another hundred hours or so of flying time. About then word was circulated around Oakland Airport that the British were recruiting for the RAF. It was sort of sub-rosa though, because they really weren't allowed to. I had applied to the Army Air Corps and had been turned down, and I was really eager to fly with an air force—any air force. So I signed up. I took some exams from a retired Air Corps major who was a medico down in Berkeley. Then I was assigned to Bakersfield (California) July 1st, 1940."

And Carroll McColpin (Nos 71, 121, and 133 Eagle Squadrons) remembered: "Most of us were in the 19–23 age bracket. At twenty-seven I was one of the oldest. Each of us had his own reason for joining. Some had washed out of flying school because of the rigid discipline. Others simply could not take the long routine in the U.S. services to become military pilots,

when they were already experienced aviators. For myself, I reasoned that since I had flown most of my life and knew there was going to be a global war, why not start flying for England, a country that needed help and believed in our precepts of democracy, and one that would be our ally soon in any case? I knew America was on the verge of war. When the Battle of Britain started, I decided that I couldn't just stand by and do nothing."

So, they and dozens more like Godfrey, Gray, and McColpin went to England to be Eagles, and later, when the U.S. did enter the war, were transferred from the Eagle Squadrons into the United States Eighth Army Air Force, in the Fourth Fighter Group. There, Johnny Godfrey met, and soon teamed up with, Don Gentile, another American Eagle who had come to England via the Clayton Knight Committee and Canadian flight training.

A native of Piqua, Ohio, Dominic Salvatore Gentile was the son of Italian imigrants who had settled in the United States in 1907. Captivated by airplanes and anything to do with aviation, Don worked in his father's tavern to earn money for flying lessons and eventually persuaded his dad to help him buy an airplane. His goal was to become a fighter pilot and, beginning with his junior year in high school, he tried to apply for the Army Air Force, the Navy and the Marine Corps, all of whom turned him down. Later, however, the Clayton Knight Committee helped him in the direction of the RCAF and the military flight training he wanted. In November 1941, he received a commission as a pilot officer in the Royal Air Force. He was off to England.

Like Gentile six months before him, John Godfrey was posted to Eshott, Northumberland, near

Above: Major Don Gentile on his P-51C
Mustang, Shangri-La; right: John Godfrey and
Don Gentile at Debden.

Newcastle. There they had both become familiar with the marvelous Vickers-Supermarine Spitfire fighter plane. At the OTU (Operational Training Unit), an Intelligence officer had told them: "We will teach you how to fight an air battle. That is your business and you must know it well. But this knowledge is worthless unless you act decisively, instinctively, and fast. We will teach you all the ramifications of the Spitfire and its armament. When the course is completed, you will be able to go find the beggars and clobber them out of the sky."

Don Gentile finished the OTU course and was graded above average as a pilot and average in gunnery. Assuming one had good qualities and at least an average rating or better as a pilot, the one characteristic that could separate him from the herd was truly exceptional eyesight. It was that particular gift that made John Godfrey special, that and his determination and ability to take full advantage of it and practice diligently to refine it. He reasoned, as did all the of greatest fighter aces, that the ability to see the enemy early and crucially, before that enemy spotted him, was absolutely vital to success in the fighter pilot business. Shortly after completing the OTU course, Johnny, together with Bob Richards, applied for and was granted transfer to the U.S. Army Air Force. America was in the war by now and the three Eagle Squadrons had been reformed into the new Fourth Fighter Group at Debden. JJ transferred to the USAAF too but was posted to the 356th Fighter Group at Martlesham Heath in Suffolk. Don Gentile too became a member of the Fourth and was assigned to the 336th Fighter Squadron, as was Godfrey.

The Fourth was the newest fighter group in England, but was, in fact, the most combat-experienced and well-prepared fighter outfit in the European theatre of operations. And when it was announced that the group would soon be converting to the new P-47C Thunderbolt, it provoked an undercurrent of unease and protest at the thought of having to give up the agile, comfortable, pilot-friendly Spitfire they knew and loved. They would have to make the adjustment to the big, heavy, seemingly less capable Republic fighter. To the pilots of the Fourth, their Spitfire was a sure-footed, graceful little filly; the Thunderbolt a bullnecked, unwieldy stallion.

Grover Hall, the public relations officer of the Fourth, later wrote a book about the group, *1,000 Destroyed*: "To the 4th went the dubious honor of selection to give the Thunderbolt its combat baptism.

There were a lot of little things. The propeller on old-model Spits turned counter-clockwise, so they would have to grow accustomed to the different torque of the P-47. They liked the Spit's 20mm cannon, and saw little sense in the P-47's eight .50 cal. machine-guns. The cannon is larger and more explosive; with cannon a pilot could always see when he got strikes on an enemy plane; it gave the exhilarating feeling of tearing the German to bits. They were not impressed by the fact that the .50 cal. machine-gun bullets had much more range and that many more rounds could be carried in the wings.

"The Spit's legs were knock-kneed and close together, while the P-47's were bow-legged and wide apart like a hawk's, so it could land in places the Spit couldn't taxi. The pilots complained that the mirror and glass canopy on the P-47 made it difficult to spot enemy planes. But the chief thing the pilots abhorred about the P-47 was its great size and weight (seven tons). With their radial engines, the craft resembled milk bottles. The pilots missed the jockey feeling the Spit compactness gave. Early model 'T-bolts' had a way of giving off smoke in the cockpit, which fact all but made some pilots bale [sic] out. At first, they weren't supposed to go below 18,000 feet in combat with '47s. The pilots junked the P-47 rearview mirrors and installed Spit mirrors and bleated, 'If they had to change why couldn't they give us Mustangs instead of these things? They won't climb, they won't turn tight, they won't do anything but dive.' "

When they arrived by truck at the 336th Squadron dispersal, Godfrey and Richards were welcomed by several of the pilots. There they met Jim Goodson, commander of "A" Flight, and Don Gentile, the "B" Flight commander. In his fine book, *The Look of Eagles*, John Godfrey wrote: "Both Don and I, of course, never guessed at this first meeting how our lives would eventually intermingle. Many stories were to be written of Don, with me basking in his limelight. The descriptions of him were invariably the same—tall, dark, handsome . . . But no matter how much was written about him, no one put down on paper the true Don.

"In an era of swash-buckling, hard-drinking, carousing fighter pilots, Don stood out like a symbol of virtue. His only vice was an occasional cigar. The majority of us lived from day to day; Don was just the opposite. Every pay day most of his month's pay was sent home to be banked in his account. Don had been born of immigrant parents, and maybe for this reason an ambition boiled inside of him to prove his capabilities to the world. The hard shell about him was very seldom broken. To deviate from his appointed task seemed to him a weakness. Sometimes I was able to observe, through an occasional crack in this shell, a different Don, one who could suffer spells of depression and who knew his human limitations. These cracks didn't show very often though, and like a turtle sensing danger, Don would retreat once more into his armour. In the air, however, it was different."

It was then that it sank into Johnny. It felt like a strange exhilaration mixed with a horrible feeling of remorse. "I'd destroyed my first plane, and undoubtedly killed a man . . . I flew, unscathed, through the smithereens of what was a plane and a man, and banking sharply I cleared my tail and watched the clouds hungrily suck the falling debris into their bosom. The

Pilots of the Fourth Fighter Group in a mission briefing at Debden.

wind dispersed the fast-disappearing black cloud, and I flew alone.

Back at Debden that evening, Johnny was buying drinks for everyone in the bar when the group commander, Colonel Chesley Peterson, came in and congratulated him. "Lieutenant, could I have a word with you in private?" Johnny followed him out into the hallway. Peterson said: "I want to tell you this in private so as not to embarrass you in front of your friends. I want all my pilots to finish their tours. What you did today was very foolhardy and risky; for this reason I cannot condone it. In the future, stay with the group, and if you want to go on a bounce, make sure that somebody is with you."

Don Gentile: "Making a fighter pilot is a long business. My instructors had worked hard back home, and when I was graduated I was graded 'better than average pilot.' But flying an airplane is only part of fighting with one, and most of the other part a man has to learn in actual combat. He has to learn from his fellow soldiers, and from the enemy.

"I was lucky enough to get attached to the Eagle Squadron, in which some of the finest fighter pilots who ever lived were working—lucky enough to get into the war at a time when a man could afford to be cautious about learning and could feel his way and did not have to throw himself against the enemy and try to clout him down blindly.

"I learned a lot from the enemy, too. In the beginning we were up against Göring's Abbeville Kids, those yellow-nosed Focke-Wulf veteran big-timers. There were not many better teachers of attack and defense than those killers, and of those who were better teachers, quite a few were in the Eagle Squadron.

"There are two things a fighter pilot must have to do his work in combat and that he can't really acquire anywhere else except in combat: confidence in his ability to kill and confidence in his ability to get away when in trouble. If you feel you can kill and feel they can't kill you, then you'll have the offensive spirit. Without that offensive spirit—ability to lunge instantaneously and automatically like a fighting cock at the enemy the moment you spot him—you are lost. You either 'go along for the ride,'

as we call it when a fellow hangs back and doesn't make kills, or eventually you get shot down. I know because it took me quite a long time to build up confidence in myself, which I thought I had when I left home, and there was quite a long time when I went along just for the ride.

"I started . . . by picking the best man I could get to fly on my wing— Johnny Godfrey, of Woonsocket, Rhode Island, who doesn't like Germans. They killed his brother, Reggie, at sea, and the name Johnny has painted on his plane is *Reggie's Reply*. He means it too. The point about him is that he not only is a fierce, brave boy, but he knows his business as well.

"As he got to know Don Gentile better, Johnny came to like and respect him as a fighter pilot and as a man: "I found in Don Gentile a section leader who knew my capabilities and had faith in my eyesight. He was aggressive, which I liked, but having had so much more experience, he served as a check to my recklessness. The first two German planes that he destroyed were shot down while with the RAF at Dieppe in 1942. He had destroyed two more with the USAAF, and one more would make him an ace. He was quiet on the ground, but once he stepped into the cockpit of a plane his manner changed completely. Gone were the suppressions and fears that often plagued him, and he flew his plane with complete confidence. Teamwork when properly used was a potent offensive weapon . . . I was envious of Don's accomplishments. If I could only shoot down two more planes this month I would have accomplished in four months what had taken him much longer; this team-work idea might work out to both our advantages."

In January 1944, Colonel Don Blakeslee took over as commander of the Fourth Fighter Group. He would lead them in combat on most of their missions that year. And since the accession of Blakeslee as group commander, Godfrey had been pleased at the way the group had grown more aggressive and spirited against the enemy air force. When Blakeslee took command, most of the original Eagle alumni had left Debden, either through rotation or due to enemy action. But some of the big-name

Far left: Major John Godfrey; left" Major Don Gentile at the Debden fighter base; below: A Republic P-47 fighter in D-Day markings.

Major Don Gentile with his P-51 Mustang, *Shangri-La* at the Debden base.

Eagles remained, including Gentile, Duane Beeson, Bud Care, Steve Pisanos, and Jim Clark. Blakeslee, on assuming command of the group: "The Fourth Fighter Group is going to be the top fighter group in the Eighth Air Force. We are here to fight. To those who don't believe me I would suggest transfering to another group. I'm going to fly the ass off each one of you. Those who keep up with me, good; those who don't, I don't want them anyway."
—from the diary of 1st Lt. Jack Raphael, 336th Fighter Squadron

When he became a member of the Fourth Fighter Group, John Godfrey was twenty-one years old. It was September 1943, and he was assigned to "B" Flight of the 336th Squadron, which was led by Don Gentile. Godfrey was, in his own words, "a sort of rebellious guy at home." His mother and father had wanted him to go to college after high school, but he refused. Later, with the death of his brother, killed in the sinking of his ship by a U-boat off Greenland, the war became personal for Johnny and he vowed to shoot down as many German pilots as he could to avenge his brother.

In his first combat mission with the Fourth, a bomber escort to Essen, Germany, he flew as wingman to Gentile. That night in the bar at Debden, Don told Steve Pisanos how impressed he was with Godfrey's flying ability and especially keen eyesight. From that day on, Johnny was invariably the first of the group pilots to spot the speck that grew into an enemy plane. He was quick to realize that the smooth, eager, alert Godfrey was going to be an excellent wingman. But the free-spirited and somewhat "rebellious" Godfrey still had a thing or two to learn about being

a team player. He had come over to England to shoot down enemy planes and neither the colonel nor anyone else was going to stop him. If he chose to risk his own life that was his business. Gentile tried to persuade him that he would have to change his perspective if wanted to survive his tour of duty. During one particular mission, when he was flying Don's wing, Johnny started to see the sense in what Gentile had said to him. As a team, that day they each destroyed an Fw 190 and damaged another. The idea that teamwork was the key to success and survival in air fighting seemed to sink in during that mission, and thereafter the pair concentrated on perfecting their method as a team.

Gentile: "John and I had been separated from the others in my flight and suddenly, as we turned around to look for some of our boys, I spotted these two lone Fw 190s cruising along. I told Godfrey 'Let's go and jump these two guys before they get away.' We turned and dived on them and as we got close behind them I said to John, 'I'll take the one to the left and you take the guy on the right,' and that's how we clobbered them. After we parked our Jugs I asked John what he thought about his second kill. He said: 'Perfect teamwork. I liked it.'"

The Debden pilots lived two to a room and Gentile shared a room with Steve Pisanos, who recalled: "I believe that the January 5th, 1944, mission to Tours, France, in which Gentile and Godfrey got two more Fws, was the birth of the legendary Gentile-Godfrey team in the Fourth Fighter Group, that was to cause so much havoc for the Luftwaffe in the days ahead." Thereafter, the pair worked harmoniously together, shooting down the enemy in droves.

Steve Pisanos: "Each night, Don and I analyzed and evaluated the

mission we had flown that day, considering our mistakes and those of the bomber boys, and the excessive chatter of some of our guys over the R/T, which was something our group commander, Don Blakeslee, did not tolerate. We talked about the different tactics and techniques of air fighting, taking advantage of the sun in getting ready to jump an opponent, attacking a stationary or moving train, and the element of surprise when attacking a ground target. We agreed completely on the importance of making only one pass when strafing parked aircraft on an airdrome, because any additional passes, regardless of the direction of your approach, will inevitably draw fire from the drome defense gunners who will then be waiting for you. Don mentioned too, how he had learned to admire and respect the capabilities of other pilots in the 336th Squadron and how impressed he was with the talents of John Godfrey as a fighter pilot. He talked too, about his belief that you had to prepare yourself for air combat by studying and learning all there is to know about the rules of the game because, when you find yourself in the midst of an aerial duel, there is no time to stop and think about what you should do. If you stop to think about it, you will not have time to act. He believed that it was essential for a fighter pilot to know the capabilities of his own aircraft by heart, as well as those of the machine his enemy is flying."

In January 1944, Don Gentile downed his fifth enemy aircraft and became an ace. Johnny got his fifth kill on March 8 and attained the same status. In his combat report for that day, Don stated: "I was flying Red I when the combat started; at the time Lt Godfrey and I were alone and we went down to break up a head-on attack on the lead box of Forts by a large gaggle of Bf 109s. There were about fifty 109s in the area flying in twos and fours. I picked out two and we did about six or seven turns with them. Lt Godfrey got one. He had a hard time turning without flaps, but when I used them I closed in to 75 yards and clobbered him. He rolled over and went down streaming white smoke. He was spiraling out of control and almost obscured by smoke. We attacked another 109 head-on. Using combat flaps, I got line astern on him, closed to 100 yards, got good strikes and saw the pilot bale [sic] out. I then noticed two 109s flying almost abreast and close together. I told Lt Godfrey to take the one on the right and I took the one on the left. I opened fire at 250 yards and closed in until I almost rammed him. I got good strikes. The plane went down spinning and smoking badly and the pilot baled [sic] out. Lt Godfrey's [enemy aircraft]

exploded.

"Then Lt Godfrey was attacked from 4 o'clock. We turned into him and got him between us. I fired first and got strikes but overshot, so I told Lt Godfrey to take over. He got strikes but ran out of ammunition. I told him to cover me while I finished him off. His belly tank caught fire and he went down to 1,000 feet and baled [sic] out.

"During this combat, many 109s were in the area and we were able to pick the best bounces. It was the way that Lt Godfrey stayed with me in every manoeuvre that made our success possible."

Shortly after the outbreak in 1939 of the Second World War, the British Air Ministry, while wholly confident in the ability of its Spitfire and Hurricane fighters to defend Britain against the German enemy, began to realize its

need for a large quantity of fighters with far greater range. It needed at least one thousand of them for delivery by 1941 and an Anglo-French Purchasing Commission was soon formed and sent to the United States to initiate such an order. They felt that the Curtiss P-40 would meet their requirement, and tried to persuade Curtiss and other U.S. plane makers to build it in quantity production for the RAF.

One of the American firms the commission called on was North American Aviation in Inglewood, California, run by James "Dutch" Kindelberger, who discussed the request with his chief designer, Edgar Schmued, a German immigrant who had been with North American since 1936. When asked by Kindelberger what he thought of the company building P-40s under license from Curtiss, Schmued instead talked his

Below: Ralph "Kidd" Hofer; right: Hank Mills, both of the Fourth Fighter Group at Debden.

boss into designing and building a new and better fighter, an airplane that would ultimately become the P-51 Mustang, the greatest long-range escort fighter of the war and the only one capable of shepherding the heavy bomber streams of the American daylight offensive all the way to the deepest targets in Germany and back to the English bases.

John Godfrey: "Rumors had been flying hot and heavy that we were being transferred from P-47s to P-51s. We had heard a lot of talk about this amazing plane. By cutting the fire power to four machine guns and using a new type of carburetor, it was capable of 1,800-mile flights with its two [external fuel] tanks. Our P-47s had only one belly tank, which was slung underneath the fuselage. The '51s had them slung under each wing with two more permanent tanks in the wing and another just to the rear of the

cockpit.

"On February 22nd, the rumors became a fact; one P-51 landed and we were all (sixty pilots) ordered to fly it in preparation for the change-over. It was a beautiful airplane; it reminded me of the Spitfire, with its huge in-line engine. And, like the Spitfire, it too was glycol-cooled. We queued up on the plane like house-wives at a bargain sale. The time in the air was spread very thin, forty minutes was all the time I had in the air in a '51 when on the morning of the 28th the group flew to Steeple Morden in their P-47s and traded them for P-51s. The planes didn't have their auxiliary tanks on, but they were full of fuel and the machine guns were loaded. Our briefing was held on the ground among our '51s. No flying back to Debden for us, but off on a fighter sweep to France. We were familiarizing ourselves with the

plane the hard way.

"The Air Force had made no mis-take when they made their purchase of Mustangs from the North American Aviation Company. They were the hottest planes in the skies. From zero to 30,000 feet they were able to match anything the German Air Force put into the air. If the fighting spirit of the group was high before the advent of the '51, it was now at fever pitch. But horrible little bugs were plaguing the '51s—motor trouble, gas trouble, radio trouble—and the worst bug of all, besides our windows frosting up, was in our machine guns. At high alti-tudes they froze up on us; moreover, in a dogfight they were often jammed by the force of gravity in a turn. That meant straightening out before firing, a feat that was practically impossible under the circumstances. Technicians were rushed to the base to iron out our problems. The war was still going

on and the great air offensive against Germany was now in full swing, so we had to fly them, bugs and all."

In the first week of March 1944, the Fourth flew the first escorted bombing attack on Berlin, a mission that would not have been possible without the availability and capability of the Mustang, even with its early problems. The weathermen in England had got it wrong too and the conditions were deteriorating rapidly. Eighth Bomber Command aborted the mission and notified the bombers to return to their bases. Colonel Blakeslee, in the lead of the Fourth, radioed his pilots that the mission had been canceled and to return to Debden. But only about half the pilots heard the message. The rest, including Major Halsey, Captain Gentile, and Lieutenants Branes, Carlson, Dunn, Garrison, Godfrey, Herter, and Millikan, continued into a cloud formation and the weather went from bad to worse. Roaring out of the cloud, the American pilots immediately encountered a huge force of enemy aircraft, some sixty Fw 190s, Bf 109s, and Me 210s. The handful of Mustangs were caught up in the swarm and facing impossible odds. With every man for himself and no chance of working in standard leader/wingman elements, it quickly turned into the most frightening moments of Johnny Godfrey's career as a fighter pilot. It was only his willingness and ability to throw his Mustang through the encounter in the most ham-fisted manner that allowed him to survive it. And in doing so, he substantially increased his dogfighting knowledge and skill. Godfrey: "I freed myself from the first mad onslaught and headed for the deck. I heard some of the other boys on the R/T trying to reform. I felt more secure in the knowledge that some of them had

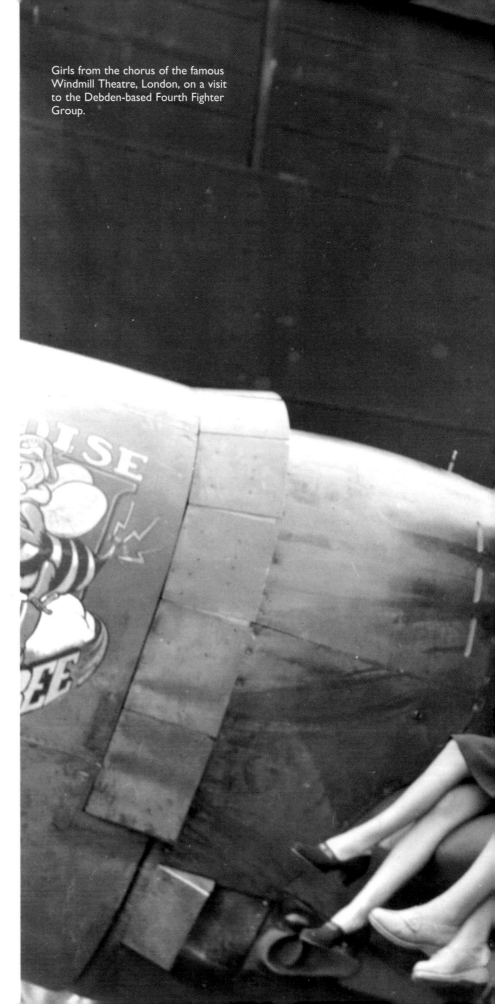

Girls from the chorus of the famous Windmill Theatre, London, on a visit to the Debden-based Fourth Fighter Group.

A P-47D Thunderbolt fighter at Duxford, England, this one was formerly with the Fighter Collection based there.

escaped also. I started climbing back to see if I could spot them. At 28,000 feet I leveled off without seeing a plane in the sky. Calling on the R/T for their positions, I failed to receive any answer. A plane was approaching, and because of its long nose I thought it was a Mustang. Turning into it I received a shock; it was neither a Mustang nor an Me 109, but a new Focke-Wulf; its long nose was the latest improvement of the famed Fw. These planes with the longer noses were rumored to have more horsepower than their predecessors, and were capable of giving a Mustang a rough time. We met practically head-on and both of us banked our planes in preparation for a dogfight.

"Around and around we went. Sometimes the Fw got in close, and other times, when I'd dropped my flap to tighten my turn, I was in a position to fire; but the German, sensing my superior position, kept swinging down in the turn, gaining speed and quickly pulling up, and with the advantage he would then pour down on my tail. Time was in his favor; he could fight that way for an hour and still have enough fuel to land anywhere below him. I still had 400 miles of enemy territory to fly over before I could land. Something had to be done. Throwing caution to the wind I lifted a flap, dove, and pulled up in a steep turn, at the same time dropping a little flap. The G was terrific, but it worked, and I had the Jerry nailed for sure. Pressing the tit I waited, but nothing happened, not a damned thing. My guns weren't firing.

"By taking this last gamble, I had lost altitude but had been able to bring my guns to bear while flying below the Fw. With his advantage of height he came down, pulled up sharp, and was smack-dab on my tail again. The 20mm cannon belched and

I could see what looked like golf balls streaming by me. A little less deflection and those seemingly harmless golf balls would have exploded instantly upon contact with my plane.

" 'Never turn your back on an enemy' was a byword with us, but I had no choice. Turning the plane over on its back, I yanked the stick to my gut. My throttle was wide open and I left it there as I dove. The needle stopped at 600 miles an hour—that was as far as it could go on the dial. Pulling out, I expected at any minute to have the wings rip off, the plane was bucking so much. The last part of my pull-up brought me up into clouds. I was thankful to have evaded the long-nosed Fw, for that pilot was undoubtedly the best that I had ever met. I saw no other planes on the way home and had to wait until landing to hear the fate of my buddies."

Gentile: "A group of Me 110s, Do 217s, and Ju 88s passed underneath us coming head-on. I rolled over starboard and started down but was bounced by ten Fw 190s, which Lt Millikan, doing an outstanding job, engaged and drove away from me. I dove on down and got on the tail of a twin-engined plane, but my canopy was so badly frosted over that I couldn't see anything. I was scared of hitting him so pulled up and turned my defroster on and when the canopy started to clear there was a 110 right beside me and firing at me. I broke away and was again bounced by three Fw 190s. I turned into them, met them head-on, and they just kept going. I then bounced the Do 217 in a port turn, fired a short burst above and astern, and my gun sight went out. I pulled up, gave another short burst and saw strikes. Just then two 190s flashed past, one on each side so I pulled away.

"I asked Lt Millikan if he was with

me and he said 'Hell, I'm fighting ten Fws,' so I figured he needed help. I tried to gather the odd Mustang I saw floating around, telling him to join up. Then I saw a gaggle beneath me going around in a pretty good formation. I half rolled and went down, but suddenly found myself in the midst of twelve to fourteen 190s, with no Mustangs around. I did a port, steep climb turn full bore. On the way up,

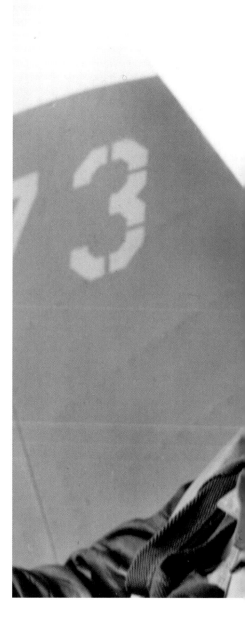

an Fw 190 was in front of me. I pulled around and put him under my nose and fired a burst. I then repeated the process, saw some pieces come off and the pilot bale [*sic*] out."

AN EIGHTH AIR FORCE FIGHTER BASE, ENGLAND—April 10—(INS)—Col. Don Blakeslee's Fourth Fighter Group today broke all records for the European Theatre of Operations, boosting their score to 403 in a strafing mission over France. The colorful, hard-flying group swept into first place in the fighter sweepstakes, gaining the triple-tiered crown for having the highest scoring group, the number one ace, Capt. Don Gentile, and the record for 31 kills in a single mission.

Below left: Captain Vermont Garrison of Mt Victory, Kentucky, with his P-47 Thunderbolt fighter at Debden; below: General Dwight Eisenhower, Supreme Allied Commander, Europe, presenting awards to Major Don Gentile, center, and Colonel Don Blakeslee.

Ray Wild, standing center
d his B-17 crew at Podington,
orthamptonshire, England.

RAY WILD

Lieutenant Raymond Wild was a B-17 Flying Fortress pilot with the Ninety-second Bomb Group (H) stationed at Podington, Northamptonshire, in the autumn of 1943. He participated in missions against German targets during the most difficult and danger-ous period for the American bomber crews in the European Theatre of Operations of World War II. For the U.S. Eighth Army Air Force, Mission 115 was the second Schweinfurt raid, an attack on the industrial center where the majority of ball bearings were made for the German aircraft industry. For Ray Wild it was the third mission of his amazing tour of duty.

Wild: "We arrived at Podington in September 1943 and they had us shoot some landings right away. At Podington the runways were built right into the farm, and the farmer was still farming it. The farmer was there, and the farmer's daughter was there. He'd be farming when we left on a raid and he'd still be farming when we came back.

"They checked out our crew and assigned us to the 325th Squadron. They had a wall with names on it—twelve missions, fourteen missions—and MIA, KIA. None of us knew what that meant. They showed that to us and then took us to the ready room. There was a certain kind of dust in there; I don't know what the hell it was, but I sneezed eleven times in a row. We took our crew out flying for-mation for a short period; how long depended on their need for replace-ment crews to fly missions.

"One of the first things I did when I got to England was to look up an

RAF pilot who had been a classmate of mine during training in the States. We went out and had a couple of beers with some of his buddies. They thought that we Americans were out of our minds. They had tried daylight bombing and it just wasn't feasible. They said we'd get the hell shot out of us. They were right. On the first few raids we did get the hell shot out of us. But those Limeys did something that sure would scare me—night bombing. They'd come in over a tar-get a minute apart, one guy this way, another guy from another point in the compass. This would scare me to death. They had tremendous intestinal fortitude. They were also realistic in that they couldn't bomb by daylight. Those Lancasters were built to carry bombs, and not to protect them-selves, while we could, or thought we could. So long as we stayed in tight formation, we could throw a lot of lead out in the right direction at the right time.

"The frightening times of a raid for me were before takeoff and after you got back down. In the ready room you were with a bunch of other guys, and you were wisecracking to ease the tension. I remember that just before my first raid—the one where you are really frightened to death—I went into the john in the operations tower. Didn't have to go, but just went in and sat on the john. That was when the song "Paper Doll" had just come out and somebody had written all the words on the wall. Just through nothing but being nervous I sat there and memorized those words. The mission that day, 8th October 1943, was a rough one. I was being sent out as copilot with Gus Arenholtz, a helluva nice guy who later became a good friend of mine. They were sending me to be oriented by him. We took off in the foulest weather

Left: General Frank Armstrong, on whom the character of General Frank Savage in the film *Twelve O'Clock High* was based; bottom left: Gregory Peck, who played Savage in the film; below right: The crumbling flying control tower at the former base of the 401st Bomb Group, Deenethorpe, Northants.

and, when we got over the middle of the Channel, and I was really scared, Gus said to me, 'Take it a minute.' I said 'Okay,' and took the wheel. We were flying in formation and he reached down and put on flak gloves, a flak suit, and a flak helmet, and said, 'Okay, I've got it.' So, I reached down and said, 'Where the hell is mine?' He said, 'Didn't you bring any? I said, 'You're breaking me in.'

" 'Well, don't worry about it,' he said, '. . . it's gonna be an easy raid.' I said, 'Okay, I'll hold it a minute,' and he replied, 'No, I've got it.' And I said, 'No, I'll hold it. You take that stuff off. If it's gonna be an easy raid, give it to me.' 'Like hell I will,' he said.

"Our ship got back with a two-foot hole in one side, one engine shot out, three of the six elevator control cables shot in two, and our radio operator wounded. Because we got back safely and all the crew survived,

from then on I sat in that same john every morning, and I still know every word of "Paper Doll."

"Many of my mission memories are associated with particular odors. The first time it hit me was the first time in that ready room. It was damp and musty—had probably been that way for months. Then, when you went into that briefing hut, and the briefing officers checked you out, you would always smell shaving lotion on those

guys. It bothered the hell out of me. You had these heavy boots, heavy pants and jackets, and you opened them up and there was body smell then—not really unpleasant, but not pleasant, because it was connected with the raid. Then we might sit, waiting in the airplane for thirty, forty minutes, and there was a heavy smell of gasoline, but there was a ready room smell in there too, every time. I guess it was the smell of fear. On the runway, and for the first thousand feet or so, there'd still be the gasoline, and the smell of burnt cordite from the Channel on, from the test-firing of our guns. The cordite smell was so strong that you'd keep asking the top turret and ball turret gunners to check the engines because you thought of fire. There always seemed to be a kind of haze in the airplane, from the guns going off. But it probably wasn't true.

"Everything was connected to emotion, I guess. You hated to get up in the English fog. You hated to be briefed. You hated to be told where you were going. You wore heavy woollen socks 'cause your feet perspired and they turned to icy-cold sweat if you didn't wear them. You climbed in the truck and they took you over to the officers' mess and there was the odor of powdered eggs. God damn, that was horrible! If you were flying you got fresh eggs.

The guys who weren't flying ate the powdered eggs.

"The cold at altitude was incredible. The gunners wore electric suits—the blue bunny suits—which they plugged in at their stations, but sometimes the suits would short out and they were in trouble. Up front we had a heating unit which didn't work too well. At altitude you were nervous and frightened and you would perspire. If you didn't wear gloves the

Below left: Part of a surviving Nissen hut at the former Deenethorpe base of the 401st Bomb Group, 8AF; below: A U.S. Army Air Force booklet for air gunners; below right: General James Doolittle, Commander of the Eighth Air Force from January 1944; bottom: The B-17G *Dog Breath* of the 452nd Bomb Group based at Deopham Green, Norfolk.

throttles would freeze and get slippery. I used thin kid gloves. They also had fleece-lined gloves, but they were impractical for flying. Coming back, we'd take off the oxygen mask and smoke a cigarette, and there was that smell, and always the cold sweat smell, until we got back on the ground. But after we landed, there was no gasoline smell, no cordite, no sweat, nothing that wasn't nice. It was all connected with fear and non-fear, I guess."

Center top: A B-17 bomber gas cap found near a hardstand at Grafton Underwood, Northamptonshire, home of the 384th Bomb Group in WWII; far right: An 8AF bomb group jacket patch; below: The waist gunner positions on a B-17 Flying Fortress bomber.

October 14, 1943. Wild: "Believe me, I never hope to go through anything comparable to this again and live to write about it. If anyone were to sneak up behind me and bellow 'Schweinfurt' I would probably run screaming down the road. Those of us who were lucky enough to return know how much body and soul can endure. When you have enough people trying to take that last little hold you have on life away, you really get down to some honest to goodness fighting and will use any measures to strengthen your grip.

"My friend, James McLaughlin, said to Budd Peaslee, who was the Eighth Air Force commander in the air for this Schweinfurt raid, 'I don't think we're going to make it.' In his heart I think he knew he was going to make it, or he wouldn't have gone. If someone tells you to get in the airplane, you're gonna bomb Schweinfurt today and you're not coming back . . . Jones is, Smith isn't, Brown isn't . . . hell, you wouldn't go! Who would? Two out of three of you guys will not be coming back today. You'd look at the guy on your left and the guy on your right and you'd say, 'You poor guys.' Pride made you get into the airplane, more than anything else. Certainly not bravery.

"You were either stood up or stood down. Stood down meant get drunk because you weren't flying the next day; your name wasn't on the list, which would go up at nine, ten, or eleven p.m. the night before a raid, depending on when the word came through from Eighth Bomber Command [Pinetree] at High Wycombe. You went based on the weather over Germany, not the weather over England. Your weather could be really bad, but if the weather over there was good for visual bombing, you went. Sometimes, of course,

it wasn't good for visual bombing and you did it by radar.

"Normally, we would be awakened at, say, 1:30 a.m. When you got up and knew you were gonna fly a mission, you hadn't slept all that well, Some will tell you they had, but they hadn't. The deepest sleep you'd get was five minutes before they would wake you. We'd put on our coveralls and shoes and then flying boots over them. We wore our fur-lined flying jackets in to breakfast, as well as our 'hot-shot Charlie' hats—the garrison hat with the grommet removed to give it the 'fifty-mission-crush' look. They would tell us that the truck would be outside in twenty minutes, and we'd go eat breakfast at 2 and be at the briefing about 2:45. Then we'd go down to the ready room and the navigators went to their own briefing. The enlisted men went to their briefing, which was much shorter than ours. After that our copilot went down with the crew and shaped them up for the mission; made sure they all had their Mae Wests, parachutes, and other gear; that the plane was ready to go. He had two to three hours on his hands in which to check things. The pilots just hung around the ready room, shootin' the bull and hoping the mission would be scrubbed and they wouldn't have to go. Then we'd be told that takeoff would be at, say, 5 a.m.; the start engines and taxi times when we all went out and weaved around through the taxi strips, following a certain airplane according to the order for takeoff.

"When your turn came to take off, you lined up so that one guy would take off from this side of the runway, and the next guy from the other side. That way you had a better chance of avoiding each other's prop wash.

"The B-17 was a very consistent, dependable airplane. You went down the runway, you hit a hundred and ten, you pulled the wheel back, and it would take off. You'd come in over the fence at a hundred and ten, it would stall out at ninety-two, ninety-three. Shot up or in good shape, they were pretty consistent. It was amazing, but it was also a tremendous feeling of comfort.

"The throttle quadrant on a B-17 is shaped like an H with a closed top. The top two are the outboard engines; the bottom two are the inboards. There is a circle a few inches in diameter where half on the right is the number three engine, bottom right is the number four, top left is number one, and bottom left is number two . . . so you could just roll 'em going down the runway.

"And boy, did it take punishment. It would fly when it shouldn't fly. There was no reason for it to fly and it would fly. Everybody in the '17 knew that the plane would get back. If they could stay in it, and stay alive, they knew they'd get back. We all had tremendous confidence in the airplane. My crew were convinced there was no other airplane like the B-17, and I could be the worst pilot in the world and they were convinced I was the best. What they were doing, I guess, was convincing themselves that they'd get back.

"I called every B-17 I flew *Mizpah*, Hebrew, meaning 'May God protect us while we are apart from one another.' The name was actually only painted on the first airplane I flew. I flew a total of nine different B-17s. If you got one shot up, maybe they'd repair it or use it for spare parts, and the next day you'd be flying a different airplane. It could have flown ninety-two missions, or this could be its first, but the ground crews were so great, it didn't make much difference.

"They would truck us to the ready room, where we would yak, go to the john fifteen times and pick up our Mae Wests, and parachute back or chest packs. Most of the pilots and copilots wore chest 'chutes because movement in the airplane was so restricted. You kept your harness on but stowed your 'chute right behind your seat so you could grab it and hook it on just before you had to get out. You also picked up your flak suit, which was like a baseball catcher's chest protector. Every time we would change planes, my engineer would change the armor plating under the seats because most of the flak would come up from underneath. A lot of the wounds were castration, so we'd put armor plating under our bodies. Some guys wore a flak helmet. I didn't. I took the inner lining shell out of an infantry helmet and used that. I carried a .45. All the officers . . . the bombardier, navigator, pilot, and copilot, had .45s. The chief engineer had a tommy gun and the other five enlisted men had carbines. We took them, but I was against them because we had been told that if you got knocked down, you shouldn't give up to civilians because they had probably lost a mother, father, brother, sister in a bombing raid and would pitchfork you to death. If you saw military and were caught, you should give up to them.

"There isn't anybody that wants to get killed. You'd go into the briefing room and you'd get the weather officer, intelligence, flak positions, and so forth. They'd pull the curtain back and you'd see this line going to the target and you'd think, 'Oh, boy, I'm not going on this. This'll kill me. What I'll do is, I'll wait a while and then I'll go on sick call and get out of it.' Then you'd go down to the airplane and you'd figure, 'Well, I'll go on sick call later.' And then you'd see everybody

get in their planes and you'd know they were just as frightened as you were, and you'd think, 'What the hell, I'll go about a hundred miles and find something wrong with the airplane.' But they had this tradition that an Eighth Air Force sortie never turned back from the target. So, in the end, you didn't dare turn back.

"On instruments, we took off a minute apart; visually, thirty seconds apart. On instruments, we would take off and go straight ahead until we broke clear. The weather reports were real bad because we had so little information. The Germans weren't gonna give us any. But most of the time, the reports were fairly close, and when we broke through, we did a circle and looked for the colored flares of the squadron and group leaders. We'd form on the squadron first, then the squadron commander would form on the group.

"We were off to a comparatively early start on Thursday, October 14th. We reached altitude and got over the French coast. Somehow, we failed to pick up the low group of our wing. As we were lead wing, the Colonel decided we had better fall in with another group. We did a three-sixty over the Channel and, seeing a 'bastard group' of fifteen planes ahead of us that didn't seem to be attached to anyone, we just tagged along with them. We picked up enemy fighters at just about the time our own escort had to leave due to fuel consumption. We had P-47s and they could only take us a certain distance in, and you could see the Hun fighters circling out there, waiting for our escort to leave. From that moment it was an unbelievable horror of fighting. For at least three hours over enemy territory, we had between 300 and 400 enemy fighters shooting tracer[s] and rockets

Opposite page: Eighth Air Force bomber air crew.

8AF bomber aircrew A2 painted flying jackets.

The cockpit of a B-17
bomber showing engine
throttles, propeller con-
trols, and instrumentation.

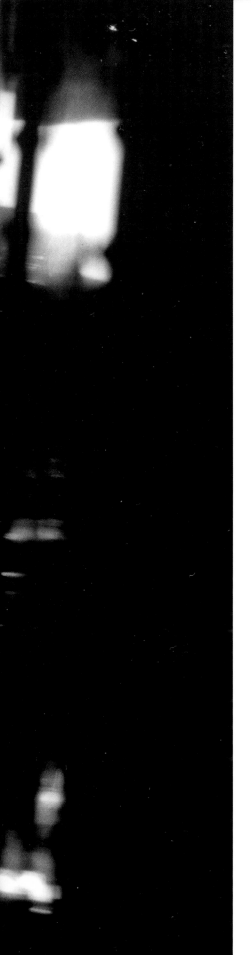

at us. You could see those rockets coming. They were about eighteen inches long, and when they hit they would explode and set a plane on fire. Some twin-engined jobs at about a thousand feet above us were dropping bombs on the formation. There was no way they could aim at any one bomber—they were just dropping bombs into the group. And they were dropping chains or cables to foul our propellers.

"We were riding Ray Clough's left wing when he got hit. He dropped out and, I believe, burst into flames because twenty seconds later I looked under my left wing and saw a burning wing floating lazily downward. Oliviero was riding Brown's wing when Brown got hit by a rocket and disintegrated, a great sheet of flame and then a hole in the formation.

"At this point I took over the lead of the second element just prior to going over the target. Major Ott was riding on three engines and had to drop behind. I never saw him again. Even over the target, the enemy fighters came on through the flak. It was one of the few times they did that. They were really first team, those guys. They had guts and they were damned good fliers. They'd come in close, and if you straggled by as much as fifty yards, you'd had it. You'd get hit by three or four guys. The German fighters normally attacked you from the best position they could get in, usually from above. At Schweinfurt, most of them came in from the front, forty or fifty abreast. They'd peel off and another forty or fifty would come in from the front, fire, and peel off. They were close . . . real close.

"I called out 'friendly fighters' by mistake one time. I couldn't identify an airplane. God, I was horrible at it. Gene Logan, my copilot, was real good at identifying them. Many times they

would barrel-roll through the group. About ninety per cent of the time they weren't shooting at individual airplanes, just going through and pouring into the group . . . unless you straggled. Then they would come get you. The one exception was our lead plane. They always tried to knock down our lead plane because there were usually only two bombsights in a group, the leader and the deputy lead plane, and I guess they knew it. I'd look up and see these guys coming in and I'd scrunch down behind the skin of the airplane, which seemed like about 1/10,000th of an inch thick. They'd come in and the rate of closure would be between 400 and 500 miles an hour and I would always wonder if they were gonna break or collide with us. They'd come in shooting. You could always see the wings 'blinking' and you knew they weren't saying 'Hello Charlie' in Morse code. It was worrying because you'd think, if they hit my wingman then I've got to do something about that, but at the same time my oil pressure is up and my cylinder head temperature is up, and I just have too many things to worry about to be frightened . . . except I WAS. That rate of closure. Boy, they were coming in through a hail of lead, and they'd keep on coming. You'd see a wing break off one and he'd spin in, but the rest of them kept on coming. 'My God, he's not gonna break off, he's not . . .' Then, finally, he'd barrel-roll and go over or under us. They pressed home real good.

"The most frightening thing about the enemy fighters was not so much their pressing of the attack, but knowing that, having pressed in once, they would peel off, go out to the side, line up, and press in again!

"As soon as you hit the coast of France, the first burst of flak would be right off your nose. I don't know how the hell they knew where you were going to be, but they knew. A flak burst that was a near miss produced a sound like pebbles bouncing off a tin roof, and you'd hear a crackling through the airplane where you were getting shrapnel coming through. In an actual hit, you wouldn't be there. With a near miss, there would be a 'whoomf' sound, and the blast effect moved the airplane. Mostly, we only heard the sound of our own engines, except for the whoomf of the near-miss flak bursts, and of course, the sound of our guns firing. They were REAL loud. Going over the Channel, I'd tell the crew to clear their guns, and this would really break you up! Especially the chief engineer's turret right behind us. We'd *feel* that. There was a lot of conversation over the intercom . . . twelve o'clock level, three o'clock high, etc. You couldn't talk across to your copilot without using your throat mike. It was even tough when you were down low. The B-17 engines were slightly behind you, but boy, they were noisy.

"The German 88mm guns which were, I think, mostly used for flak, were tremendously accurate, just fabulous. They used two types—predetermined and box barrage. In barrage there'd be a flock of guns and they'd shoot at one spot in the sky. You had to get through that spot when they weren't shooting. Emden, Kiel, Wilhelmshaven, Munich, Berlin . . . I think they did both [types] at all five of those targets. But Schweinfurt was murder. I'm sure they shot barrage there because they had so damned many guns. The German fighters stayed pretty much out of the flak, but at Schweinfurt they did come through it. It was one of the few times they flew through their own flak, but they were probably under orders. They were expending themselves. There

was no reason for it, really.

"Evasive action? I don't think you can do it against flak. Certainly not against the barrage type. Where are you going to go? Off the target? You can't win, except through luck. Now, for the group as a whole flying up to a flak barrage, if the leader says 'Use evasive action' as the group is starting to get hit, and the group turns off a bit, that's evasive action, but I don't think that the people in the low squadron would believe it. Still, for the group it's the best thing you can do.

"That indeterminate flak that was coming up, there was nothing you could do about it. This was something that was gonna happen. It was impersonal as hell.

"The main thing was, the lead bombardier did a beautiful job on the target. You were flying on the code of the day, to be at certain points at a certain time . . . the Initial Point and then the Mean Point of Impact. You had to fly straight and level for six or seven minutes. You flipped on the automatic pilot and the plane flew wherever the bombardier aimed his bombsight. He was flying the plane, really. If the bombing altitude was to be 25,000 feet and the speed 150 indicated, all you did was control the throttles and altitude and he controlled the direction. There was no evasive action. The point was to drop the bombs on the target, and the Germans knew it.

"About three minutes after dropping our bombs we got hit in number three engine. Due to loss of the prop governor control, we couldn't feather it and we began to sweat. We had to use maximum manifold pressure and 2,500 revs to stay in formation. A flak burst just off my side of the nose cracked my windshield into a million pieces. A piece of flak about an inch long and a half inch wide was right in

A Lockheed P-38 Lightning fighter, factory-fresh, in WWII at the Burbank, California, plant.

line with my face, but fortunately we had a bullet-resistant windshield and it stuck in the glass. I had the engineer dig it out for me after we landed.

"We limped home with the formation as far as the Channel and started to let down into the nearest field. We got into Biggin Hill, southeast of London. Seven Forts set down there and they were all shot up. Several had wounded aboard and one had a dead navigator. We had fifteen holes in the ship and only about sixty gallons of gas left.

"There were always runways somewhere in the neighborhood. If you were coming back from a raid and in trouble, needing a field in a hurry, or if you were in soupy weather and couldn't find one, you'd just fly a circle while saying 'Hello Darky' three times, and give them the code and call letters of the day on your radio. Then this English voice would come on and say 'Hello, Yank. How was it?' He'd be kidding you about it but within sixty seconds he'd have you on radar and would say something like 'Fly 270 degrees for ninety seconds, then left for 30 seconds on 180 degrees, and there will be an airfield right under you.'

"The papers said we lost sixty Forts on this Schweinfurt trip. At one time all you could see were parachutes and burning airplanes. But then, we knocked a little hell out of them too. My crew got two fighters, giving us a total of three. After Schweinfurt, I thought the rest of our missions would seem easy."

B-17s of the 8AF 390th Bomb Group bombing a target at Marienburg, Germany

With the end of the war in Europe, many American bomber crews departed from their English airfields for the last time, Often, they were waved off by grateful villagers they had come to know during their tours of duty.

FORDE
Dec 1940

"SAILOR"

Group Captain Adolph "Sailor" Malan
commanded No 74 Squadron, RAF
Fighter Command and No 19 Wing.

SAILOR MALAN

In the weeks ahead of the Battle of Britain, the first great air campaign in history, the German Air Force was ordered to eliminate the British Royal Air Force to make Adolf Hitler's Operation Sea Lion, the Nazi invasion of the British Isles in World War II, possible. The Luftwaffe—the air arm of Hitler's Third Reich—began the Battle with a phase that involved a series of dive-bombing attacks on Allied shipping in the English Channel as part of an attempt to stem the flow of food, munitions, and war supply to the British early in the war. The effort was mostly unsuccessful and the primary attentions of the Luftwaffe were soon shifted to attacking British seaports and the Chain Home radar sites located mainly along the south coast of England.

While conducting these raids, the Germans incurred substantial losses in the course of this phase, but still managed to increase their attacking aircraft strength from around one hundred to more than four hundred per raid. But the return on their effort was again proving insufficient to their requirement and the Luftwaffe, under German Reichsmarschall Hermann Göring, redirected its attacks in August of 1940 with the aim of destroying the aircraft and airfields of RAF Fighter Command, the primary targets being Manston, Kenley, Hawkinge, Biggin Hill, Tangmere, and Martlesham Heath. These attacks produced rather more impressive results with severe damage and significant casualties in some cases, but all of the airdromes were soon fully repaired and operational. The German inability to knock out these vital targets then led to a further continuation of the Battle in a new series of intense and ferocious bombing raids that were concentrated on British cities and industry.

Throughout the fifteen-week period of the main Battle, the area of London and the southeast of England was the territory of No 11 Group, RAF Fighter Command, under the control of the New Zealander Keith Park, Commanding Officer. In much of that time, Park's routine included a "dawn patrol" in which he climbed into a Hurricane fighter each morning to inspect the damage done the previous day. Park: "It was burning all down the river. It was a horrid sight. But I looked down and thought: 'Thank God for that' because I knew that the Nazis had switched their attack from the fighter stations, thinking they were knocked out. They weren't, but they were pretty groggy."

At a certain point in July, early in the Battle, there had been a lull in the air fighting. The WAAFs whose rakes plotted the positions of approaching enemy aircraft on the large map table at RAF Hornchurch in Essex, could do nothing but wait for the German Air Force to do something. Finally, with little warning, the lull broke as the station Tannoy loudspeakers erupted into alerts. Ground personnel were ordered to quickly arm and fuel the Spitfires of No 74 Squadron, whose pilots had been lounging in deck chairs on the grass by their dispersal. Now, beneath the bright blue skies of this rare English summer, theirs was a mixture of anticipation, trepidation, and gut-wrenching excitement.

The Hornchurch controller, Ronald Adam: "One of the most beautiful sights was to see against the evening sky the navigation lights of a homing squadron in tight formation. Round and round the aerodrome they would wheel, this twinkling cavalcade, the softer shade hiding the malevolence of their aspect, the dew falling, the flowers closing, and the deep rich hum from these flashing comets up above. The leader's voice would call, 'Red Section, break away, Go!' and section by section would peel off, until, floating out of the sky, the last three would touch down, and then cars and tenders would arrive and deposit outside the Mess their cargoes of tired pilots ready for their supper, their game of billiards or of cards, and deep sleep before 'readiness' once more as the last stars began to shine more wanly in the sky before dawn. It had a queer air of unreality, with battle far away and these lads dropping out of a peaceful sky with bullet holes and shell holes disrupting the extraordinary toughness of their aircraft, with their hair clogged and matted with the heat of their flying helmets, and still with a faraway look in their eyes of great distances and ever-present strain . . ."

The German Air Force had lost 488 aircraft by August 18, with most of the crews killed or captured. The RAF lost 220 aircraft, with many of the pilots saved. Then there was a five-day lull in the fighting during which the Germans regrouped before resuming their bombing raids on Britain, now with smaller formations and increased fighter protection. On August 20, British Prime Minister Winston Churchill addressed the Commons in what may have been his most famous and memorable speech: "The gratitude of every home in our Empire, and indeed throughout the world, except in the abodes of the guilty, goes out to the British airmen, who, undaunted by odds, unwearied in their constant challenge and mortal danger, are turning the tide of world war by their prowess and by their devotion. Never in the field of human conflict was so much owed by so many to so few."

In Kent and Middlesex counties, residents were witnessing a magnificent spectacle high above their fields and hop gardens, an elaborate white tracery of vapor trails, like chalk on a blue board. The fighters of the Luftwaffe and the RAF spun, twisted, and fell in the course of hundreds of aerial combats.

Adolph "Sailor" Malan was thirty years of age during the Battle of Britain; old for a fighter pilot, but his maturity brought leadership and a firm authority. The Battle produced many airmen of considerable skill and accomplishment; high achievers who made their mark in one of the most memorable and demanding campaigns in military history. Only a few of these men, however, distinguished themselves in such a way as to become legends in their own lifetimes. One of them was South African Sailor Malan. Sailor: "How did we feel? Of course,

we had our tails up. At that time the Luftwaffe seemed to be running on an endless belt—the fellow you knocked down yesterday seemed to be back [the] next day asking for another wallop. We were not without fear. The fellow who wasn't didn't live long. We couldn't see behind us and the Hun was everywhere, ready to spit his guns. Yet fear and intense physical danger and the discomfort of battle were more than compensated by the very positive feelings nearly all of us had of satisfaction at being the only human beings who were able to stand between Hitler and world freedom. We knew that any day we might be shot down to death, but I will swear that this feeling of being the only spearhead, the only instrument between German domination and democracy was the one that kept us going and beat the Luftwaffe. It gave us all an elation that far transcended all else . . ."

When Malan was given command of No 74 Squadron, one of the first things he changed was the basic formation the squadron flew. As long as he had been in the RAF, the peacetime air force had flown set formations based on standing orders and precedent. The basic element in Fighter Command was a section of three aircraft, with four such sections comprising a standard twelve-man squadron in the air. The problem with the three-man section was that the Numbers Two and Three were kept so busy concentrating on flying formation on their leader that they could not possibly keep a watchful eye out for enemy aircraft. Unless all eyes were free to scan the entire sky for the enemy, no one in the squadron was safe. As the RAF fighter ace Robert Stanford Tuck put it: "I figured it out darn quick that the 109s were coming at us 'whoomph'—just like that, all in loose formations and

Below: K5054, the Spitfire prototype, at Eastleigh Airfield, Southampton, in 1936; right: Messerschmitt Bf 110 heavy fighter which, like the Spitfire, flew for the first time in 1936.

we were flying all this jammed-in, odd numbers, which was absolutely hopeless. No freedom of action at all. You were concentrating because of the possibility of collision, when you should be looking around at what was going on everywhere else. I eased them out into pairs when I took command. Copy-book formation stuff was hopeless."

While flying and fighting in Spain during the Spanish Civil War, the fighter pilots of the Luftwaffe had seen the wisdom of flying in two-man section elements and had continued to perfect such tactics in Poland and France. Sailor knew that three was wrong and two was right. He knew too, from the lessons of the First World War that the advantage of height in air combat was vitally important and by the time of the Dunkirk evacuation in May 1940, he had the Tigers of 74 Squadron meeting their German enemy at heights

of 20,000 to 24,000 feet over and behind that part of the French coast, one reason why members of the British Army on the beach there frequently asked "Where is the RAF?" They were there but were operating so high that they could not be seen or heard by those on the beaches. Malan influenced Stanford Tuck and Al Deere and the three of them steadily changed the RAF's accepted rules of air fighting.

It was when No 74 Squadron was posted for a short rest and training period to RAF Kirton-in-Lindsay, Lincolnshire, in mid-August 1940, that Sailor began developing his famous *Ten of My Rules for Air Fighting*, which he later refined while in command of the Central Gunnery School at RAF Sutton Bridge. His "rules" quickly became the classic tenets for the fighter pilots of the RAF and were pinned up in many fighter station crew rooms

around England. Those pilots with the good sense to follow them often outlived their colleagues who ignored them. Sailor: "Generally speaking, tactics in air fighting are largely a matter of quick action and ordinary common-sense flying. The easiest way to sum it up in a few words is, apart from keeping your eyes wide open and remaining fully alive and awake, it is very largely governed by the capabilities of your own aircraft in comparison with that flown by your opponent. For example, in the case of the Spitfire versus the Me109F, the former has superior manoeuvrability, whereas the latter has a faster rate of climb. The result is that the Spitfire can afford to 'mix it' when attacking, whereas the Me109F, although it tends to retain the initiative because it can remain on top, cannot afford to press the attack home for long if the Spitfire goes into a turn. Obviously, there are a lot of factors involved which must

govern your action in combat—such as the height at which you are flying, the type of operation in which you are engaged, the size of your formatio, etc. There are, however, certain golden rules which should always be observed. Some are quite obvious whereas others require simplification.

1. Wait until you see the whites of his eyes. Fire short bursts of one or two seconds, only when your sights are definitely 'ON.'
2. Whilst shooting think of nothing else, brace the whole of your body; have both hands on the stick; concentrate on your ring sight.
3. Always keep a sharp lookout. 'Keep your finger out.'
4. Height gives you the initiative.
5. Always turn and face the attack.
6. Make your decisions promptly. It is better to act quickly even though your tactics are not the best.
7. Never fly straight and level for more than thirty seconds in the combat area.
8. When diving to attack always leave a proportion of your formation above to act as a top guard.
9. INITIATIVE, AGGRESSION, AIR DISCIPLINE, and TEAM WORK are words that mean something in Air Fighting.
10. Go in quickly—punch hard—get out!"

Successful fighter pilots are definitely a breed apart. Believe it or not, for better or worse, they are equipped with qualities and characteristics that separate them from the pack, enabling them to excel in the strange art and science of hunting and killing in wartime. One historian compared the born fighter pilot to a greyhound: ". . . when he sees the enemy he goes for him, regardless of the odds." And another one wrote: "Temperament, condition, and a good constitution

certainly matter." And another: "A pilot's fitness was not the same as a boxer's. A pilot worked on his nerves. His physical condition only had to be good enough for him not to think about it."

Sailor considered himself fortunate in his mixed parentage: "My father is descended from French Huguenot stock, freely mixed with Dutch blood, but my mother was English. The French are opportunists. The Dutch have vigor, tenacity, and patience. The English have more courage than any other people in the world."

Sailor believed that there are certain qualities a fighter pilot must have. In the First World War, fighting in the air was, in his view, largely a matter of individual courage. Flying ability and good shooting helped, but usually the aces were men who waited until they got in close and who took terrific chances. It was different in the Second World War, he felt. Courage was a minor talent. No man was braver than the next. The civilian fighters in London—the air raid wardens in Coventry or Plymouth—these men did things under fire which the fighter pilots could only regard with awe. A fighter pilot didn't have to show that kind of courage. Unreasoning, unintelligent, blind courage was, in fact, a tremendous handicap to him. He had to be cold when he was fighting. He fought with his head, not his heart. Sailor believed that "there are three things a first class fighter pilot must have. First, he must have an aggressive nature. He must think in terms of offense rather than defense. He must at all times be the attacker. It is against the nature of a Spitfire to run away. Second, both his mind and body must be alert and both must react instinctively to any tactical situation. When fighting, there is no time to think.

Third, he must have good eyes and 'clean hands and feet.' His hands and feet control his plane and they must be sensitive. He can't be ham-handed. When one's Spitfire is ambling along at 390 miles an hour, a too-heavy hand on the stick or a too-heavy foot on the rudder will send one into an inadvertent and embarrassing spin. One's hands, feet, mind, and instinct must function as well whether one is right side up or upside down."

Disciplined, aggressive, sensitive, and clever, Sailor embodied the qualities he defined as essential in a successful fighter pilot. His stated opinion on courage aside, he was easily among the best of the bravest, most confident warriors developed in the Royal Air Force. He was well liked and attracted friendships, but was not sentimental and shied away from sentiment.

Sailor's capacity for living in the present greatly helped him to survive in combat. He did not allow himself to be overly influenced by his imagination. He knew his Spitfire intimately, became as one with it in the air, and trusted it completely in combat. He worked hard to increase his ability to withstand the effects of G-forces, advancing from a point of four Gs—the average blackout threshhold—to more than five., where a target object takes on a grey, even tone, eliminating the brighter colors which, at speed, are a distraction. He expected the same discipline in his pilots. In a spiral dive, acceleration and centrifugal force make a 180-pound man feel like he weighs over 1,200 pounds. Sailor would admonish his men "I am setting my engine at four boost. If you can't keep up, go home."

He differed in other ways from his fellow pilots. In addition to being older by five or more years than most of them, and more experienced of

Part of the flying kit of the typical RAF fighter pilot in the Battle of Britain period.

A Royal Air Force fighter pilot on the wing of his Spitfire in World War II.

life and war, he was not one of the long-haired, weekend flier types; he had no particular interest in sports cars and was never an habitual user of current air force jargon. Wholly focused and thoroughly professional, he knew where he was going and why, and stood out from the rest like the polished, tested, air leader he was. Sailor was one of what author Lovat Dickson referred to as "the tough, practiced men who had come up the hard way, who, unlike the average Oxford undergraduate were not flying for aesthetic reasons, but because of an instinctive knowledge that this was the job for which they were most suited . . ."

After his rural South African upbringing and harsh merchant fleet cadet training, Sailor liked the "democracy" he found in the air force, the fulfillment in the rank, seniority, and tradition. He had a

special affinity for the people who did the real jobs, the pilots who flew the Spitfires and Hurricanes in deadly earnest, for whom killing in that situation was a profession. He appreciated their skill and deadliness. Aggressive, assertive, unemotional in the business of air fighting, like most in his line, he never saw any of the men he killed.

One particular experience Sailor recalled was flying with one of his newer pilots, a bright, well-educated, and spirited young man who, for some reason, was unable to properly maintain his position in the flight: "He was a boy born to be killed. You knew, or felt, that it was only a question of time before he was picked off. Yet the cruelest thing of all would have been to tell him to drop out of the flight and recommend him for an OTU (Operational Training Unit). He had lots of guts. He struggled hard to be a good pilot. But everything was against him. It wasn't just a matter of the aircraft he was flying, although youngsters are expected to take the older machines. He flew with me several times. I felt partly responsible for him. But you can't risk the striking force of the squadron for an individual. We were on a patrol one day with this boy flying No 4 astern. Suddenly, looking round, he had gone. We never saw what happened. A Jerry must have sneaked up behind and picked him off."

Sailor had a lot to give his young pilots and found them eager listeners whose respect and admiration for him was evident when he told them that, "as the sole object of taking off in a British fighter on an operational sortie is to knock down one or more Huns, the ability to shoot accurately is a major requirement, and that a lot of tripe has been said about the cunning of the so-called expert fighter pilot."

The more combat experience he

had gained, the more Sailor was convinced that the chief qualities required in an expert fighter pilot are: "1. The ability to shoot; 2. Reasonable flying accuracy; 3. Quickness in reacting to any situation; 4. Good eyes. Not everyone is naturally gifted in these ways. But a reasonable pilot, through diligent practice can make himself a good marksman. Having learnt to fly accurately, it's your business—if you are in the RAF—to make yourself proficient in applied flying. To a fighter pilot this means chiefly the ability to handle your aircraft like a gun platform."

He told them that whenever they went up they should take every opportunity of practicing forms of attack, curves of pursuit, and aiming the machine at targets, both moving and stationary, to practice throwing it into quick turns, onto clouds, or any moving target within reason. They would also find that, by constantly whipping the machine into turns at high speed, and half-rolling and pulling out, one will increase one's blackout threshhold.

He said that the ability to react quickly is more instinct than applied. Some pilots are fortunate there. More often than not, the man who nips in quickly without a second's delay wins, because with the speed of a modern aircraft, a few seconds' start is a tremendous advantage.

Good eyesight, he told them, is also a gift, but eyes can be trained. The best training for a fighter pilot's eyes is to practice looking at distant objects. Whenever you've a spare moment at dispersal point, instead of gazing vacantly into space, or reading a book, spend as much time as possible looking at distant objects and spotting details.

Superior height, he said, always gives you the initiative, so always strive for it. Many pilots, who admit this, have deluded themselves that in combat other factors are just as important. One fallacy, for instance, is that if the aircraft is designed to give its best performance at a certain height, a pilot feels this is the best height to fly. He is thus throwing aside the essential fact that an enemy aircraft, with perhaps fifty mph less speed, can obtain the extra speed as well as the initiative by starting a fight from a few thousand feet higher with a diving attack.

He cautioned them to always cruise at high speed, and to train members of their formation to cope with a leader who is giving them the minimum amount of extra boost and revs to play with. It is better to cut down your radius of action and increase your performance. If the strategy demands that you operate at low cruising speeds and weak mixture in order to gain your objective, the strategy is faulty.

While a lot has been said about fighter formations, in Sailor's opinion,

a fighter formation is only effective if it combines maneuverability, flexibility, and simplicity. A fighter formation must never, never dive to the attack without leaving at least one-third of its strength above as a top guard. This rule never is to be departed from.

Strict air discipline, he reminded them, is essential for successful combat. It is good for teamwork and therefore morale. Team rules should be few and simple, but rigidly enforced. After each engagement, a post mortem should be held. One definite rule he stressed is that the unit should fight in pairs. No 2 should always remain with his leader, not as an attacker, but as a rear guard while the leader attacks. A junior officer acting as No 2 can thus gain experience for the time when he is a leader.

He said that nearly all attacks began to develop along a curved path of pursuit. This may not sound important, but it is vital. If the attack-

er is seen, it is generally important to avoid a stern chase, for obvious reasons. With a certain amount of practice, the fighter pilot can soon learn when to commence his turn into a target. In order to prevent a stern chase, the curve-in must be started from well before the beam, if the target is doing a reasonable speed. An attack can be delivered on a much faster aircraft provided the turn-in is started in plenty of time.

Once having closed the range, he continued, it can be decided whether to attack with deflection or to swing round to the dead-astern position. For the two main types of target (i.e., fighter and bomber), the problems are not at all similar. The bomber is most vulnerable from a head-on attack, and has its armor and armament astern and on both sides. The fighter, on the other hand, has its armor forward and aft and its armament generally forward. With the bomber, surprise

is difficult, whereas with the fighter it is comparatively simple. It will be unprofitable to attack bombers from anywhere except from ahead and the flanks, particularly when they are flying in formation, which is their chief form of protection.

Sailor added that, when attacking bomber formations, the best plan is to deliver the initial attack from ahead, provided strategy permits. After that, one should attempt to break up the formation if this has not already been achieved by the head-on attack. With the fighter, the head-on attack should be avoided at all costs and, if surprise can be achieved, attack with overtaking speed from below and astern, firing being withheld until extremely close. Resist the impulse to fire at any range except harmonized or closer ranges. Range estimations, although one of the fighter pilot's chief enemies, is the cause of most of the "probables" and "damaged," and is a very simple matter

Far left: Group Captain Sailor Malan at RAF Biggin Hill; left: Kath Preston, landlady of the White Hart pub in Brasted, Kent, the popular haunt of the pilots of RAF Biggin Hill nearby.

to overcome. Always aim at the top edge of the target.

Sailor felt that the German fighter pilot paid a lot of attention to tactics—a good fault, but unfortunately for Hitler, he seemed to lack initiative and "guts." His fighting was sterotyped, and he was easily bluffed. Part of his reluctance to stay around and mix it was due to his aircraft being less maneuverable. The German pilot insisted on using the same old tricks, without any imagination. For instance, he would detach a pair of decoys that dived in front of a British formation, hoping someone would be fool enough to follow them, and the others could then do a surprise bounce on the rest of the Brits. Despite many warnings, some of our pilots have been caught by this.

He said that the old saying from the First World War, "Beware of the Hun in the sun" is truer than ever because: 1. The Hun seldom attacks from any direction except the sun; 2. The mod-

ern machine, with its clean lines and good camouflage, is more difficult than ever to spot against the sun; and 3. Modern high speeds allow less time than ever before your opponent has you in range. Never forget that the man who knocks you down in air combat is usually the one you don't see. If the enemy is in range, so are you.

Sailor carefully explained that a fighter pilot should approach the problem of teaching himself how to shoot and fly in exactly the same way as he would learn to use a shotgun. First, your shotgun instructor shows you a shotgun—the various parts of it, its trigger action and safety gadgets, so, your flying instructor shows you your airplane and explains the flying controls and knobs in the cockpit. You handle the shotgun and get familiar with it. The instructor shows you how to hold it and use it, so that you can get used to the feel of it. You learn to fly and how to handle your airplane so that

you can get your sights in the right place in the quickest possible time.

When you can handle the gun instinctively, your instructor will tell you the ways and wiles of ducks, and how you can find them. So, you will learn the tactics of fighter operations and how to fight. Your Spitfire is nothing but a gun with a couple of wings and an engine to keep it in the air. Your job is to use it as a gun and fly it as a part of you with your attention outside of it, until you have something in your sights, when your whole concentration is along the sight and on the target.

Sailor: "Unless you take a tremendous grip on yourself on operations," he warned, "you're certain to fire at twice the range you ought to. It feels easier to shoot when the range is great; the contrast between the size of the enemy aircraft, from the speck it was when you first saw it, to the size of it when you feel close enough to shoot, makes it look as if it is two

TEN of MY RULES for AIR FIGHTING

1 <u>Wait until you see the whites of his eyes.</u>
Fire short bursts of 1 to 2 seconds and only when your sights are definitely 'ON'.

2 Whilst shooting think of nothing else, brace the whole of the body, have both hands on the stick, concentrate on your ring sight.

3 Always keep a sharp lookout. "Keep your finger out"!

4 Height gives <u>You</u> the initiative.

5 Always turn and face the attack.

6 Make your decisions promptly. It is better to act quickly even though your tactics are not the best.

7 Never fly straight and level for more than 30 seconds in the combat area.

8 When diving to attack always leave a proportion of your formation above to act as top guard.

9 INITIATIVE, AGGRESSION, AIR DISCIPLINE, and TEAM WORK are words that MEAN something in Air Fighting.

10 Go in quickly – Punch hard – Get out!

Above: Sailor Malan's air combat rules are believed to have saved the lives of many RAF pilots in the Second World War and since.

NOTICE
OWING TO THE PRESENCE OF PETROL & OIL
NO PERSON SHALL SMOKE
USE MATCHES OR LIGHTERS
WITHIN THE AREA ENCLOSED BY THIS BAR

hundred yards away when it is six hundred. Sheer determination alone will make you hold your fire. There are two ways of judging range. One is to learn by means of the range bars, or by knowing how much of the ring the target should fill at, say, three hundred yards—and never shooting while it is smaller. The other is to notice, at a particular range, how much detail of the aircraft you can see—the crosses, the oil streaks, the pilot's canopy—and never shoot when you see any less.

"Whatever kind of attack you are making, always bring your sight up to the target from behind it, and carry it through the target along its line of flight until you reach the correct deflection; then fire. Don't hold the sight ahead and wait for the target to meet it. Otherwise, it is impossible to hold a steady aim without skidding and making the shooting phenomenally difficult for yourself. This is infinitely more the case with an airplane than it is with a shotgun, because an airplane is slower to handle and you are firing a continuous burst. Even with a shotgun you must always swing through from behind . . . "

Spitfire final assembly area in the Vickers Castle Bromwich plant near Birmingham in the Second World War.

MERLE OLMSTED

Up to this point all the high achievers in this book have been airmen—pilots mostly. Now for something different. Master Sergeant Merle Olmsted was a Mustang crew chief with the 357th Fighter Group based at Leiston, Suffolk, England, in the Second World War. The Leiston base was just eighty miles across the North Sea from the German-occupied Netherlands. Merle remembered the daily grind on his fighter station: "Dawn had not yet broken through the swirling mist at Leiston. It is January 1945, and many of the 1,500 men of the fighter group and its supporting units are still secure in their cots. Many others, however, have been awake all night as numerous shops and offices at the field required twenty-four-hour manning.

"Among those awake, and hopefully alert, are the CQs [Charge of Quarters], an old Army term for the noncommissioned officers who man every unit's Orderly Room during off-duty hours. It is a job that rotates among all the unit's NCOs. With the coming of daylight, the three squadron CQs go forth from the Orderly Room to rouse the pilots and ground crews. They had been jarred from late night lethargy by the phone call from Group Operations which, at some time during the night had received a teletype field order for the coming mission from 66th Fighter Wing. The Field Order, originating from Eighth Air Force Headquarters, spelled out the mission objectives, units involved, bomber routes to the target, fighter rendezvous times and locations, radio codes, and all other information needed for the unit to play its part in the continuing air assault on Germany.

"As the CQ goes from hut to hut the routine is the same. He steps through the blackout door, flips on the light switch, and says in a loud voice: 'Briefing 0700, maximum range, maximum effort.' Normally, only the wake-up time varies depending on the pilots' briefing time. In the case of the pilot' barracks, he wakes only those scheduled to fly today.

"The first item on the agenda is breakfast at the big consolidated mess hall or the officers' mess. From there, it is off to the flight line via GI truck, bicycle, or on foot, a distance of about one mile. With the crews on their way to the Mustangs huddled under their covers, and the pilots drifting into Group Briefing, the day's activities begin to accelerate.

"For centuries large military bases have tended to be self-contained cities. Leiston airfield, USAAF Station F-373, like dozens of other Eighth Air Force installations which sprawl across East Anglia, is no exception.

Below: Former USAAF Master Sergeant Merle Olmsted.

April 11, 1944. Lt Mark Stapleton and the pilots of the 364th Fighter Squadron, 357th Fighter Group, were engaged in a fierce air combat over the city of Leipzig, Germany: "My guns jammed after each short burst, but thanks to an experimental hydraulic gun charger that had been installed in my plane, I was able to clear the jam and fire again. My guns jammed and were cleared at least seven times. I overran the enemy aircraft and Lt Sumner closed and observed hits on the enemy aircraft, which crashed and exploded."

"The 1,500 men (and half a dozen women who run the Red Cross Club) provide all of the usual town services and a few others of a more warlike nature. The mission of these 1,500 men is to place a few to as many as sixty-five P-51 Mustang fighter planes and their pilots over Europe every day if ordered to do so, to enable them to take on the German military and win World War Two. Everything on the station revolves around some ninety Mustang fighters and their pilots.

"These few pilots, and some 900 others, are all members of the USAAF's 357th Fighter Group—the Yoxford Boys, who have been in residence for about one year. The point of this piece is to tell something about the daily routine on an American fighter base in World War II England, from the perspective of the ground crews. It is worth noting that the 357th is among the three highest-scoring fighter groups in the Eighth Air Force.

"January 1945 has proved to be the coldest, and one of the most difficult, months for flying weather the group experienced. For eighteen days of the month, the ground and runways were either frozen or covered with snow and ice. On the 14th of the month, a date which has since become known as 'the big day,' the 357th became engaged in a great air battle in the Berlin area and was credited with thirty-five and a half enemy fighters shot down, the highest one-day score ever among U.S. fighter groups.

"Today we have left the ground crews on their way to their individual aircraft. It is not always obvious to those outside aviation (and to some in it) how critically important quality maintenance is in the operation of airplanes. In military operations it can mean the difference between success and failure, and the spectre of aircraft and crew loss due to mechanical failure is always uppermost in the minds of the ground crews.

"In the 357th, there are two levels of maintenance, the flight line crews assigned to individual aircraft, and the hangar crews which handle heavy maintenance such as engine changes. A third, higher level on the Leiston base, the 469th Service Squadron, does the more complicated jobs that the squadrons are not equipped to do.

"When ground crews are mentioned, which is seldom, the reference is usually to the crew chiefs. Most Eighth Air Force fighter units assign three men to each airplane. Besides the crew chief (usually a staff sergeant), there is an assistant crew chief (a sergeant or 'buck sergeant') and an armament man (a corporal or sergeant). Those selected as crew chiefs are usually in their twenties, or the very elderly—in their thirties. Unless

Below: A restored P-51D Mustang in the paint scheme of the 357th Fighter Group, 8USAAF in WWII; right: The manufacturer's identification plate of a Mustang Merlin engine.

one is on 'other duty,' both the crew chief and assistant arrive at their aircraft at the same time.

"Their first duty is to remove the cockpit and wing covers and the Pitot tube cover. Then the propeller is pulled through its arc a few times and the preflight inspection is started. The P-51 is remarkably simple. Nevertheless, the preflight, as laid out in the manual, is quite lengthy. Most of it consists of visual inspections, many of which have been completed during the postflight inspection the day before. All reservoirs are checked for fluid level, coolant, hydraulics, battery, engine oil, and fuel. An inspection is always made under the aircraft for coolant leaks, which frequently occur due to temperature changes. It is often difficult to tell coolant from water, but touching a bit of the fluid with the tongue will reveal the difference, as coolant has a bitter taste (and is poisonous if con-sumed in quantity).

"If all visual and servicing checks are satisfactory, the engine run is done, using the battery cart to save the airplane's internal battery. Because the seat is rather deep (to accommodate the pilot's dinghy pack), a cushion in the seat helps one to reach the brakes and to see out from the cockpit. Now the brakes are set and the seat belt fastened around the control stick to provide 'up elevators' during the power check. The flaps are left down, the fuel selector is set to either main tank, the throttle cracked open, and the mixture control set to the idle cut-off position. After yelling 'Clear!' to be sure no one is near the nose of the plane, the starter switch is engaged); the P-51 has a direct-drive starter), along with engine prime. As soon as the cylinders begin to fire, the mixture control is moved to 'run.' The propeller is already in full increase rpm for the warm-up. Various additional checks are now carried out, including checking that the engine oil and coolant temperature instruments are registering 'in the green.' The engine is run up to 2,300 rpm and the magnetos are checked. With each mag off, the maximum allowable rpm drop is 100. The propeller governor is also checked at this rpm. The maximum rpm is 3,000, but this is for takeoff and is not used on the ground run.

"After the engine is shut down and everything has checked out okay, it is mostly a matter of waiting. The fuel and oil trucks cruise the taxiway and all tanks are topped off after the run. Now the windshield, canopy, and rear-view mirror are all polished—for the tenth time today. The armament man has long since arrived and charged his guns, so all aircraft on the field have 'hot' guns long before takeoff. The gun switches in the cockpit are off, of

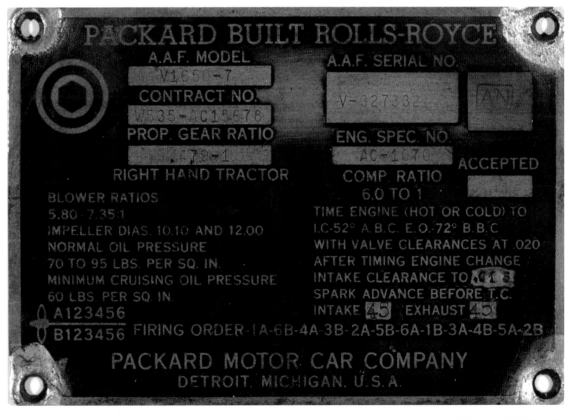

course, but occasionally one has been left on and the pilot gripping the stick could fire a burst, terrifying everyone within range, including himself.

"The pilots usually arrive fifteen to twenty minutes before engine start time, via an overloaded jeep or weapons carrier. After the pilot is strapped in with the help of the ground crew, his goggles and windshield are given a final swipe. Engine start time comes and sixty Merlins cough into life around the airfield hardstands. Then the wheel chocks are pulled and, with a wave of his hand to the ground crew, each pilot guides his fighter out to the proper place on the taxi strip in a snakelike procession toward the active runway.

"The ground crews, and everyone else in the airfield area, seek a vantage point to watch the takeoff—always an exciting event. The sight and sound of sixty or more overloaded Mustangs getting airborne is impressive.

"Much of the weight the planes are carrying today is represented by two long-range fuel drop tanks, so vital to the success of the U.S. fighters in Europe. Most of these tanks are made of paper composition units, each holding 108 U.S. gallons and built in huge quantities by British companies. They are installed on the wing racks for the next day's mission the night before and are filled at that time. During operation they are pressurized to ensure positive feeding at altitude, by the exhaust side of the engine vacuum pump. The piping for this and the fuel flow is rubber tubes with glass elbows which will break away cleanly when the tanks are dropped. Even though the drop tanks are pressurized, it is necessary to coax fuel into the system during the preflight. After switching to the drop tank position, the engine will often die, and the selector switch must quickly be put back to 'main' and then to 'drop tanks' until they feed properly. On the mission they are always dropped when empty, or earlier if combat demands it. With all fifteen fighter groups operating, Eighth Air Force fighters can require 1,800 drop tanks per day.

"At midday, while the mission aircraft are out, the line crews are in a state of suspended animation. It is mostly free time, time to attend to laundry, read the squadron bulletin board to see when mail call was, and to see if your name has appeared on any unwanted, but unavoidable, extra duty rosters. There is also time to drop into the Post Exchange for a candy bar, and to take in noon chow at the big consolidated mess hall.

"Regardless of what they have been doing while the mission was out, the aircraft ground crew always sweat out the return of their particular airplane and pilot, and when both return safely, it is a great relief.

"Whether a crew has a close relationship with their pilot depends on several factors—how long they have

Below: WWII pilot's goggles; right: A U.S. bomber aircrewman leaving the equipment hut and heading for his aircaft.

The B-24 Liberator bomber *Arise My Love and Come With Me* with its crew at the Horsham St Faith base of the 458th Bomb Group near Norwich, England.

been together, the pilot's general attitude towards enlisted men, and if he is an outgoing individual.

"Although the word 'hero' probably never occurs to the ground crews, they are well aware that it is their pilot who is doing the fighting and sometimes the dying. In most cases there is considerable affection for their pilot and they are proud of his achievements. There is always a period of depression when an aircraft and pilot fail to return from a mission, and often the cause doesn't filter down to the ground crew. In a day or two, a new P-51 arrives, and a new pilot, and the war goes on.

"An average mission of the group lasts about four to five hours and by the estimated time of return everyone is back on the hardstands. If the group comes into sight in proper formation and to the rising snarl of many Merlins, it is probable that there has

been no combat. If they straggle back in small groups, or individually, it is certain that there has been some kind of action. Missing red tape around the gun muzzles is a final confirmation.

"As each P-51 turns into its hardstand, the pilot blasts the tail around and shuts down the engine, the wheels are chocked and the mission is over—one more toward completion of his tour.

"Now he brings any aircraft malfunctions to the attention of the crew, and departs for debriefing. For the ground crews there is considerable work ahead to complete the post-flight inspection and repair the aircraft. If luck is with them, their airplane can be 'put to bed' in time for evening chow, and the workday will have come to an end. Often, though, it does not work out that way, and their jobs continue into the night.

"Our narrative has started before dawn on a dreary January day. On another day this month, two days after the group's astounding success over Berlin, Major Guernsey Carlisle led fifty-four Mustangs on a heavy bomber escort mission. He reported: 'Takeoff 0924, down approx 1600 at various bases on continent. Group rendezvoused with bombers at 1100 Zwolle at 24,000. Left bombers at 1400 at Strasbourg. Weather bad. 10/10 cloud over target. Group instructed to land on continent, returned to UK on 19th January. Lieutenant William Thompson, 363rd, killed in crash near Framlingham.'

"Thompson was a victim of the bad weather, only a few miles from home base. He is one of seven who died during January. One of these is Staff Sergeant Melvin Schuneman, a crew chief and the only 357th ground crewman to die in an aircraft accident. He was killed on the 27th in another weather-related crash, along with pilot Lieutenant Walter Corby, in the group's AT-6.

"Leiston airfield was within a few miles of the North Sea coast, and was often the first airfield seen by American and British pilots of battle-damaged aircraft. Many such cripples landed there with varying degrees of success. One of these incidents ended in a fiery spectacle in late May 1944 and is descibed here by Captain William O'Brien, USAF (Ret): 'After a mission flown in the early afternoon, I was in the cockpit of my plane, and my crew chief, Jim Loter, was standing on the wing. We saw a P-47 taxiing south to north on the perimeter track on the 363rd side of the field. The Jug was moving fairly slowly, and then he pulled into an empty hardstand just across from where I was parked. As he turned I could see white smoke

Left: In the control tower at Deenethorpe, home to the 401st Bomb Group in WWII; above: Ground crew loading .50 caliber machine-gun rounds in the wing of a P-47 Thunderbolt fighter.

When the Yanks arrived in England they brought the Jitterbug with them; The Wolf Wagon bus brought local girls to dances at the Leiston, England, base of the 357th Fighter Group.

starting to come from the lower fuselage, well back from the engine. I told Jim to try and get to the Jug with our fire extinguisher as the pilot shut down the engine. The smoking aircraft was facing to the west, and about this time its guns started to fire and the pilot was out of the plane and standing on the hardstand. It is well-known that the Jug had eight .50 machine guns. All eight were firing and believe me, that was the first and only time I'd ever heard that much firepower released. Needless to say, neither Loter [n]or I could get to the Jug, which proceeded to burn and fire its guns. I imagine everyone within four miles wondered what the hell had happened. The story I got was, the Jug pilot was short on fuel—to the extent that he might not make it, and landed at the first base he saw, planning to refuel and then proceed to home base. He got refueled all right

and was taxiing to take off when he heard a loud bang, so he pulled into the nearest hardstand. He had been doing some strafing on the way home from his mission. The loud bang was probably a 20mm or larger shell that had been lodged in the fuselage and finally exploded, possibly caused by taxiing across a rough spot, which was enough to activate the fuse. This Jug pilot was one lucky man.'

"Gunfire of a more serious nature hit Leiston airfield two weeks later. Compared with the experience of the RAF during the Battle of Britain, and the German ground crews in 1944–45, life on an Eighth Air Force airfield was a relatively safe existence. Our pilots, the only ones on station doing the fighting, faced death or capture every day, but only once in the fourteen months of wartime service did Leiston airfield encounter hostile gunfire.

"On the night of D-day (6th-7th

June 1944), the Luftwaffe struck back at the Allies in retaliation for the invasion. According to RAF records, several bombs fell on Tuddenham, and five bombs were dropped in the vicinity of Parham and Framlingham (both only a few miles from Leiston). Three night-flying B-24s were attacked and one was shot down just after midnight. An RAF 25 Squadron Mosquito encountered and shot down an ME-410 forty miles east of Southwold.

"Shortly after midnight a German intruder struck at Leiston airfield. The field, like all of England then, was blacked out, but apparently the door to the mess hall, then serving midnight chow, had been left open. Attracted by this light, the intruder fired a burst of cannon fire into the building, doing little damage other than making a few holes.

"Among those present there has always been much confusion and disagreement about the details of the incident. The type of German aircraft has never been authenticated. Group records indicate it was probably an ME-410, but two men who were outside and got a close look at it said that it was a single-engine type, an ME-109 or Fw-190. Since neither of these types was really suitable for night raids on England, it was probably an ME-410, possibly the same one shot down by the Mosquito. Sergeant James Frary made a detailed entry about the incident in his diary: 'I was standing outside the Orderly Room (I was CQ that night) and there was a red alert at the time. I heard the plane coming in low from the south. I didn't think about it being German until he reached the edge of the field and I could see him silhouetted against the sky. Just as a precaution I crouched down in front of the door. About then our AA guns started to fire. Pink tracers were going all around the enemy ship. Just as he got almost out of my range of vision he banked around to the east and cut across the communal site. It was then that he cut loose with his guns, putting three holes in the mess hall and ploughing up the baseball field with his 20mm guns. The AA fired about 300 rounds of caliber .50 and eight rounds of 40mm at him as he crossed the field. They apparently hit him as a gas cap and some scraps of metal were found later.

"Sergeant Emery Gaal, who had been working in the 364th Squadron area, recalled his view that night from the mess hall: 'Around midnight I was sitting in the mess hall with Karnicke, having a snack. We heard the plane coming and then a big boom like cannon fire. It blew a big hole just below the roof. As all of us hit the deck the benches and tables flew all over and we were hollering at the cooks to shut off the lights, which they did. After the lights went on, I found a cut on my leg

from a heavy table which had fallen on me.'

"Out on the flight line, Claude Allen of the 363rd Squadron remembered: 'It was about midnight and I had just been to the mess hall, and then to our squadron area to pick up the mail and some blankets as several of us from "A" flight usually slept out on the line near the ships. I was driving the bomb service truck and a Sergeant Van Tyne was riding with me. While returning to the flight line we stopped at the radio shack just off the perimeter track and were informed that an alert had been in effect, but as all seemed clear, I pulled back on the perimeter track toward "A" flight area. Suddenly we heard this loud drone overhead which sounded like an aircraft making a sharp turn, coming in from the direction of Leiston village, and we could see the flash from the aircraft's guns. This is when I went out of the left side of the truck, my partner out the right side. About the time we were flat on the ground, the ack-ack opened up. When it was over we found the truck, which had gone only a short distance before stopping, but did not see any damage to it.'

"The fourteen months on Eighth Fighter Command's Leiston airfield was a unique experience for the ground crews, and probably the high point of life for many. Most of us, however, did not appreciate this at the time, and wanted only to get it over with and go home. Only in later years did some realize what a fascinating time it had been, and many of us have returned several times to the now tranquil land that once housed a fighter group at war."

Right: Sunset on the Raydon fighter station.

PERSPECTIVES

Ever since the First World War, the perspective of the movie industry on films about military aviation has often tended to depart from reality. Even today, when studio committees consider the apparent merits of a proposed aerial epic, reality frequently seems to be given a lower priority than say, the profit potential in the sale of toys and other by-products related to the picture. The prevailing argument that overwhelms the case for authenticity is it seems propelled by logic such as "We'll do it with computer graphics, models, and effects," or "It will be a lot cheaper and the audience will never know the difference," and "Okay, so the script calls for our hero to be a skirt chaser. But the actual guy it is based on was and is happily married. That won't play in Peoria. Action in the air, action on the ground . . . that's the ticket!"

It seems too, that most producers tend to hire technical advisors—if they even bother—to give their air films the impression of authenticity and credibility. Mostly, though, the results reflect what appears to be a disinclination to listen to, much less take the advice of, the poor soul whose title, name, and credentials are proudly listed in the credits. And mostly, those results are an embarrassment to those involved, rather than a proud achievement.

One such example is the 1942 Universal production *Eagle Squadron.* Bosley Crowther reviewed the movie for the *New York Times:* ". . . far from the genuine drama about American fliers with the RAF that it should be, but is rather a highfalutin war adventure film which waxes embarrassingly

A Supermarine Walrus picks up a downed RAF airman in the English Channel while a Lysander spotter plane circles overhead.

mawkish about English courage and American spunk."

Produced by Walter Wanger, *Eagle Squadron* was the first major American movie about the air war that was made after the Japanese attack on Pearl Harbor and the U.S. entry into the war. Unfortunately, it trivializes the activities of the first three American fighter squadrons serving in the European war.

Several members of the Eagle Squadrons (American fighter pilots who had volunteered to serve with the British Royal Air Force), along with many prominent guests, were invited to the London premiere of the movie in July 1942. As Colonel Lee Gover, USAF, a former RAF Eagle and member of the Fourth Fighter Group, USAAF, recalled: "The film was so far-fetched from actual combat, it was really embarrassing." Most of the American pilots in attendance that evening wanted to walk out, but they felt that, as invited guests,

it would be impolite. Still, after the first half hour some of them could stomach no more and left quietly by a side door. Bill Geiger, another of the Eagles, remembered: "That movie upset everybody, and Squadron Leader [Chesley] Peterson in particular. We had been told that it would be a documentary, like *The March of Time* of those days. We all felt that we had been double-crossed. Pete was so bitter about it that he never responded to any requests for information for publicity about the Eagles from that day forward."

With the release of *Eagle Squadron*, even Quentin Reynolds, the well-known and very popular London-based American war correspondent who had often entertained Eagle pilots at his flat, and had done the opening narration for the film, was refused access to Peterson's airfield. Gover: "We were just another RAF squadron trying to do our best. We deserved, and wanted, no special

attention, because of our American background, attention that overshadowed the British and Commonwealth squadrons who were doing the same job and with whom we had to fly."

Carroll W. McColpin, Major-General, USAF (Ret): "When they had the showing at the premiere in London, they made a big deal about it, getting a lot of Eagles, as many as they could at the time, in to see it. I don't know of anybody that stayed through the picture. I'd say the bulk of us got up after about the first thirty minutes and walked out. The English were madder than hell at us . . . the protocol people, because there was supposed to be a lot of public relations and, anyway, you didn't walk out on the King, for God's sake. So, it was just a farce. Typical Hollywood. It was insulting at the time because here were the people being bombed all the time, and fighting the damned war, and then they come in with a

Wing Commander Roland Robert Stanford Tuck flew in the Battle of France, as well as the Battle of Britain.

Heinkel He-111

Junkers Ju-87

Focke-Wulf Fw-190

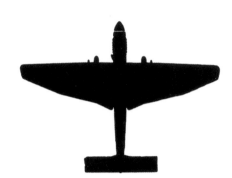

thing that's so obviously phoney even a little kid would know it."

Over the years since television has emerged as powerful competition for the cinema, most producers of aviation-related drama for that medium have shown no more interest in authenticity than their movie industry counterparts. The 1988 British production *Piece of Cake*, which was based on Derek Robinson's excellent 1983 novel of the same title, is a case in point. Many Royal Air Force pilots who were operational on squadrons in the early years of the Second World War were appalled by the representations made in the TV production. They saw little similarity between the real pilots they knew, and themselves in that war, and those portrayed in the multipart Spitfire epic. It is also the case that no Spitfires were operating in France in the period before the Battle

of Britain—the RAF squadrons sent there were flying Hurricanes, contrary to the way *Piece of Cake* represented the events. The good side: the aerial sequences were planned, flown, and filmed with wonderful graphic power; the fighter planes were worked hard and well by consumate professionals.

Still, editorial and creative license can come into play for various reasons—budget limitations, directorial whims—sometimes dictating a fudge here or a larger compromise there. Actual events re-created or real personalities represented are at times unrecognizably distorted, leaving those who lived through those events, and all who care about the accurate representation of history, wincing.

Many war films, and especially air war movies, have not found great favor among film critics over the years. After the United States entered the Second

World War, and the Hollywood motion picture industry had a year of war moviemaking under its belt, *New York Times* film critic Bosley Crowther summed up his measure of the product to date: "By and large, the general quality of motion pictures this past year has reflected the confusion and uncertainty which the war has exposed in Hollywood. Producers have plunged into purely escapist pictures or have made the war out to seem illusory by dodging it into old routines." Film historian Clyde Jeavons suggested that it was "not the nature of these early films so much to inform the public, as to stimulate . . .
to wrap the war up in attractive packaging and sell it to the people." In *Celluloid Wings*, his fine book on aviation movies, James H. Farmer wrote: "Within such a context, death for the Allies, if not for the enemy, was often antiseptic and painless. The protagonists

The cockpit of a
Focke-Wulf Fw-190
fighter.

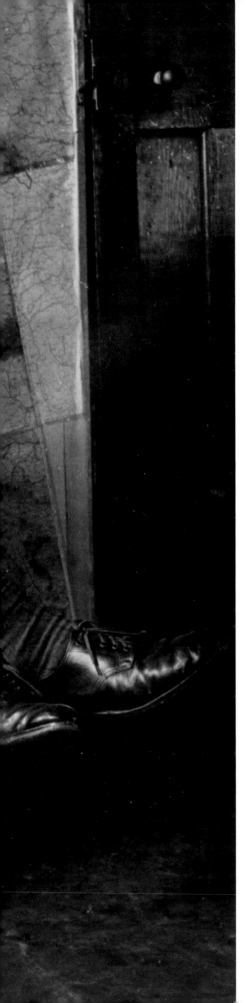

Left: Colonel Don Blakeslee, Commander, Fourth Fighter Group in WWII; above: One of Blakeslee's officers, Major Winslow "Mike" Sobanski and his P-47 Thunderbolt fighter.

A typical scene on a typical 8USAAF air base in WWII England.

were naively heroic and unashamedly patriotic. Such story lines were usually entertaining and professionally smooth but generally were far removed from the harsher reality." Crowther did feel that "the one encouraging trend has been the growing one towards actuality films [documentaries], indicated mainly in the short product and more recently in the films of the OWI (Office of War Information). Still very much on the periphery of screen entertainment, these films at least are foretelling a more thoughtful and realistic fashion in screen fare. This is the brightest prospect for films in the months—or years—ahead."

Another form of air war entertainment was the multi-episode serial that was produced for both film and radio during the war years. All pretense of reality went out the window in these little pulp fiction and fantasy potboilers mainly for younger audiences. *Captain Midnight, Flight Lieutenant, Smilin' Jack, Sky Raiders, Hop Harrigan,* and *Adventures of the Flying Cadets* had avid followings by teenage and preteen wannabe fighter pilots who, years later, would recall being inspired by these serials. Those were among the influences that led them to follow the dream of becoming fighter pilots.

Thirty-four-year-old Colonel Robert L. Scott, a high-scoring American fighter ace, had come to prominence as commander of General Claire Chennault's Twenty-Third Fighter Group, the descendants of the famous Flying Tigers in China. Now he was back in the States dictating his virtually guaranteed bestseller, *God Is My Copilot,* to stenographers at the New York publisher, Scribner's. So sought after was his still-unpublished book that Scott had been offered the then-staggering sum of $100,000. by Warner Brothers for the motion picture rights to his story.

But before accepting the studio's offer, Scott cleared the movie deal with Air Force chief General Henry H. Arnold in Washington who told him: "Make it authentic and make it faithful to the Air Force and you make them pay you." General Arnold believed in the value of showing the American public what the Army Air Forces were doing around the world. On his mind was the eventual creation of a separate and independent United States Air Force and he certainly knew the importance of effectively promoting his service.

Out in Hollywood, Hal Wallis was assigned by Warners to produce the movie version of Scott's book. The picture would star Robert Stack. Wallis hired the writer Steve Fisher to do the screenplay and Fisher wrote a first draft. Scott: "When Steve showed it to me it began to take on all these things . . . malaria [which Scott never contracted], and a Japanese pilot called

Tokyo Joe [which had nothing to do with the events of the book]." James Farmer: "Scott, a happily married man of many years, most strongly objected to the script's equally fictitious love affair." Scott: "I loved my wife and I never wanted anything like that in the movie!" After many protests by Colonel Scott, the China-based love interest was deleted from the film.

After a lengthy delay, filming of *God Is My Copilot* finally began in August 1944. The picture was released early in 1945 and the film-going public seemed to like it. The film critics, however, did not. Bosley Crowther: "Obviously Warner Brothers took the title of Colonel Robert L. Scott's war book . . . much more literally than the author did. For their rip-roaring film . . . is heavily and often embarrassingly larded with piety. For Colonel Scott's popular, vivid story of his career in the Far East has been turned by the Warners into

Left: Waking an airman for a mission; above right: Lt Col James Clark briefing pilots of the Fourth Fighter Group at Debden.

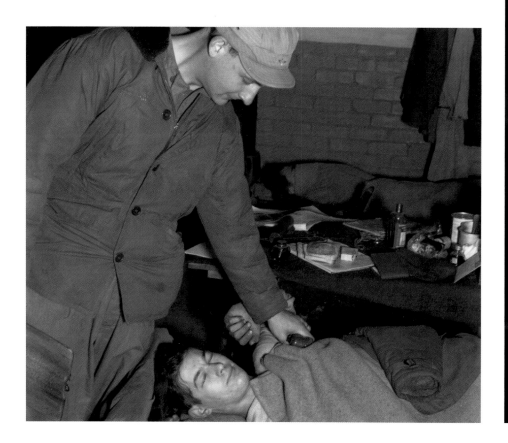

Left: Major Pierce McKennon and his Mustang fighter; below: 8USAAF B-17 bombers on a raid over Germany in 1943; right: The crew of an 8AF heavy bomber receiving last-minute instructions from their pilot; bottom center: Luftwaffe Major Gunther Rall, the third highest-scoring fighter ace in history, with 272 confirmed aerial victories; bottom right: *Gemini*, an 8AF B-24 Liberator bomber, part of the Zodiac series of B-24 nose art painted by Philip Brinkman of the 486th Bomb Group at Sudbury, Suffolk.

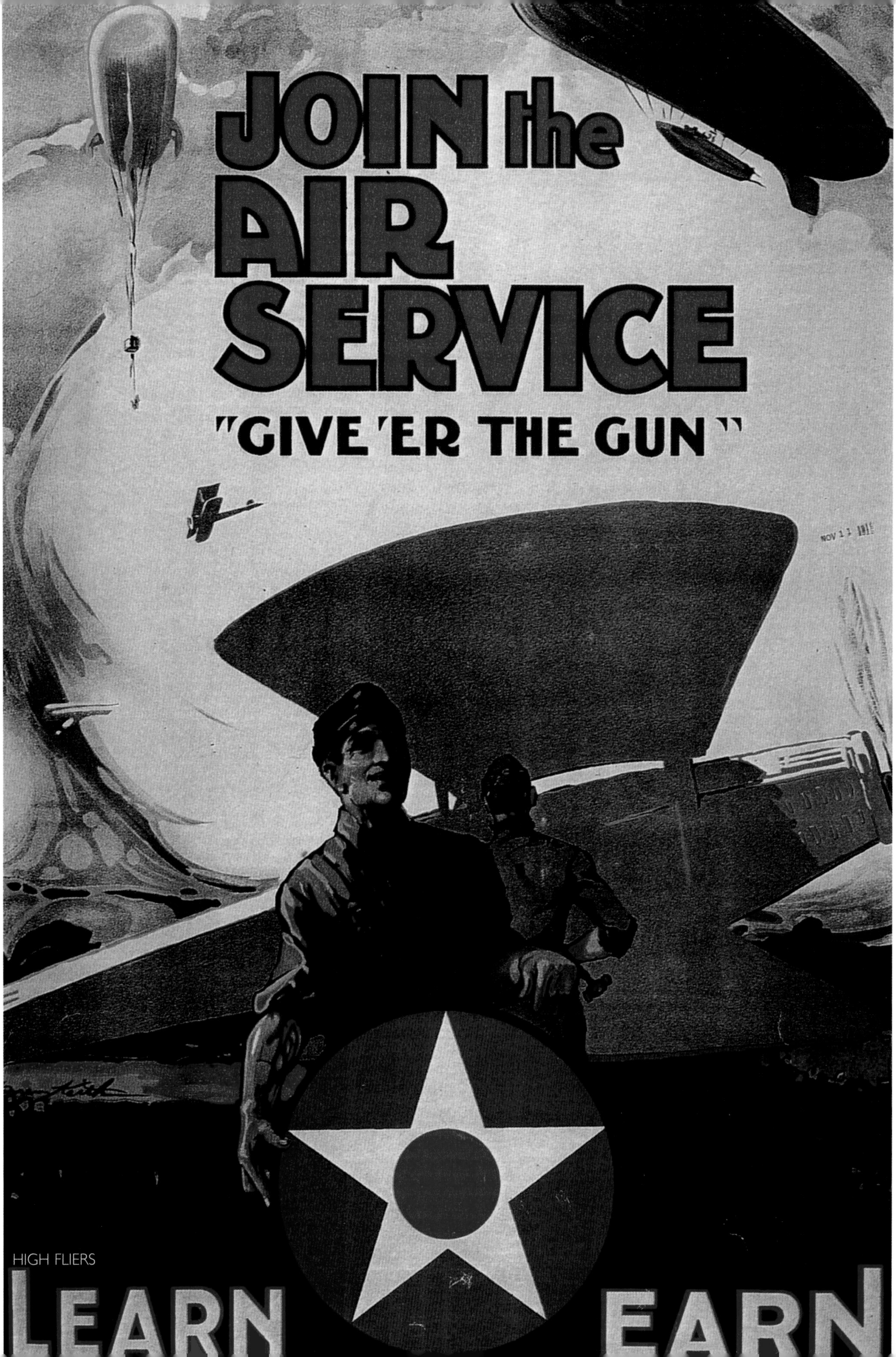
JOIN the
AIR
SERVICE
"GIVE 'ER THE GUN"
LEARN
EARN

another, rather cheaply theatrical war film." James Farmer: "Sadly much of the Peter Milne dialogue degenerates into 1942 vintage pulp fiction that pleased neither Scott nor critics—'Okay you Yankee Doodle Dandies, come and get us. I'm going to drop one of you right in Chennault's lap. Where are you gangsters? Come up and get a load of that scrap metal you sold us.' "

Scott: "Chennault had evidently sent a letter to Arnold and had used the phrase, 'I am being made to look over-sympathetic in the role projected by Raymond Massey.' So I got orders to report to the Pentagon to view the film with all the staff. And, man, I had to sit there and see that corny film in which so little is true. They made me have that malaria attack which never did happen . . . and here I sat in the Pentagon with every general and most of the admirals watching *Copilot*, embarrassed as hell. When it was all over they applauded. Arnold stood up and said, 'I see no over-simplification or over-sympathetic performance. I think it's a good picture.' And I wanted to say, 'General, what are you talking about? It never did happen like that.' And with 'Big Mike' sitting back in that P-43 saying, 'Fear can sabotage the strongest heart . . .' well, it's amazing how they make a movie!"

"The fighter pilot was a very individual person, often not represented correctly on TV or in the press. Hollywood often gave the wrong picture, and so did the UFA in Potsdam on our side. Too much propaganda; not enough truth."
—Feldwebel Horst W. Petzschler, German Air Force (Ret), formerly with X/JG51

In 1948, Warner Brothers returned to the fray with *Fighter Squadron*, again starring Robert Stack. The movie was directed by Raoul Walsh and

From Kimberley, South Africa, Squadron Leader Albert Gerald Lewis flew Hurricane fighters with Nos 504, 249, and 85 Squadrons in the Battle of Britain and after.

Bottom: A B-17G bomber after belly-landing at Bassingbourn near Cambridge; below right: Part of a B-17 instrument panel; left: One of the best bombers of the war, the Avro Lancaster ready for its takeoff on a raid into Germany.

was about a P-47 Thunderbolt outfit with "orders from above" prohibiting them from jettisoning their long-range fuel drop tanks in combat. Credibility took a massive blow again. And again Colonel Lee Gover was involved, this time as "air advisor" on the film. He remembered: "During the war they asked us to bring the belly tanks home if we could because they were scarce at first. But when we got into a dog-fight we didn't give a damn who said 'don't drop 'em.' We dropped them."

The actor Jack Larson, who played the part of Shorty, the newest and youngest pilot in the squadron, recalled: "Raoul Walsh was a very imposing personality, tough with that tough voice of his. He wore boots and riding pants and had that eye patch [he had lost an eye filming an early western]. He never really rehearsed you. He was interested in timing and dialogue and didn't deal with the actors much. He never gave me any direction except to say, 'Pick it up, kid. The scene's on its ass' and 'I could drive a truck through that pause.' "

Of *Fighter Squadron*, James Farmer wrote: "Leaving Hollywood for the last time in July, [Lee] Gover, who appears as an extra in the film's pub sequences, returned home with mixed emotions. Although satisfied with the film's flying scenes that he led in the air, Gover remained dissatisfied with much of the

The B-17 *Bomb Boogie* on her Bassingbourn base in WWII.

script. The sense of frustration would grow as veteran pilots, friends who had flown for the film and knew and felt what it had really been like in the war, were killed. For many of these men, it was their last chance to see the story told before giving their lives during the Korean conflict. Commenting on the film Gover admitted: 'I knew the movie wasn't very good, just too much Hollywood nonsense in the damn thing. I told them at the time, but no one would listen.' "

Group Captain Al Deere, No 54 Squadron, RAF on the 1968 United Artists film *Battle of Britain*: "I think they did it quite well, but the air battle was fought in the air and nothing was going on on the ground. They had to try and make something there . . . into a film. During the actual battle we never got off the airfield. There were no girl-friends or pubs. We just didn't get off the airfield. How could we? We were so short of pilots! So the filmmakers, in order to make a story, had to have a girlfriend driving up and meeting her pilot at a pub. Well, there was none of that at all. There was before and there was after, but not while the battle was on, there just wasn't. There was no relief whatsoever. Oh, we were moved as a squadron up north for a week, but that was only in order to refurbish and get some new pilots in and give them a quick bit of training, and then go back again to Hornchurch. We were on 'readiness' or we were so bloody tired, we were just dead. There was no glamour about it, really. That seems trite, but there wasn't any at the time. We didn't feel much glamour, I can tell you."

Lieutenant Colonel Robert M. Littlefield, USAF (Ret), formerly with the Fifty-fifth Fighter Group, 8USAAF: "Young men away from home for

the first time are a product of their upbringing. A few go off the deep end unless their peers intercede. As a rule, however, most young men, fighter pilots, like to drink and chase girls. I found that those I knew did not drink to excess except on a rare occasion. When in combat I flew ten days and was given three days off. I made it my practice not to drink the night before a combat mission, for obvious reasons. A good many of the young men never drank before entering the service and their drinking in the service was lim-ited. However, the older group did their share of drinking. The younger group of fighter pilots were nineteen to twenty-five years of age. The older group were five years older. Fighter pilots, by nature, are cocky, aggressive, and self-assured. How else would one go into war all by himself in a fighting machine?"

In the Second World War, Colonel John Cunnick flew P-51 Mustangs with the Fifty-fifth Fighter Group out of Wormingford near Colchester, Essex: "A fighter pilot is all balls and no fore-head. If he thinks at all, he thinks that he is immortal, God's gift to women and his airplane. On a mission, he is too damned busy to be frightened because he is alone and has to do it all. At all times he has to know where he is on the chart, set his armament switch for the occasion, scan his instru-ments and the entire sky constantly, cover his leader's six o'clock, fly his aircraft, and, at some crucial time try to relieve himself. Then, of course, he must shoot down the enemy, strafe the airfield, train, or any other targets of opportunity, etc. When the fighter pilot returns to base, that's when the bullshit starts. Yes, they were cavalier, because a fighter pilot who thought about dying usually did die."

8AF bomber crewmen after a raid.

Mustang pilot Major Don Gentile with his
crew chief at Debden, south of Cambridge.

Flight Lieutenant Charles M. Lawson, RAF (Ret): "Naturally, when you put together a bunch of young men, most [who] were between twenty and twenty-five years old, who were brought up in different countries and cultures, you are going to get a mixed bag. Most of the pilots were single, and I think those who weren't sometimes wished they were. Spitfire pilots flew in the daytime, so nights were used to let off steam and enjoy themselves. You must recognize that there was a different mindset during the war years, not just among servicemen and women, but also the civilian population. The pubs in England were great places for socializing and each squadron seemed to have its own favorite pub and the local girls knew this also. It wasn't the Hollywood-style 'eat, drink, and be merry for tomorrow we die,' but it was close to it. There was definitely a carefree attitude among the populace in those years. Of course, there were also the quiet types who preferred to stay back at the RAF base and write letters home. I wasn't one of them and I think, in retrospect, that they were in the minority. I think the average fighter pilot was a bit of a hell-raiser."

Flying Officer E. A. W. Smith, RAF (Ret), formerly with No 127 Squadron: "Derring-do was the fiction of aged fighters, often writing years afterwards—trying to depict themselves as above it all. Nonsense! We were kids, trying to get through it. We were scared to death on every mission—particularly when going in to bomb a strongpoint such as a marshalling yard. We were almost as scared of real women as we were of flak!"

Major Don Gentile, formerly with the Fourth Fighter Group, 8USAAF: "I have a habit when I am frightened of talking to myself silently—but the words are so plain in my head that it's almost as if they were echoing there with real sound.'Now, boy,' I'd say to myself, 'just take it easy and you'll be all right.' But whatever I told myself that day, I kept thinking, 'Oh, Mama!' We went along fast in a good, tight formation, like a bunch of killers going to town, I guess, but I kept sitting up there in the middle of the posse looking like one of the boys, no doubt, but thinking what a kid I was. I was twenty-one years old then, and 'what was I doing here,' I asked myself when, where I wanted to be was at home in my mother's lap."

Colonel Steve Pisanos, USAF, (Ret), formerly with the Fourth Fighter Group, 8USAAF: "When a fighter pilot walked into a pub or a hotel bar during the war, he let those inside know who he was by having the top button of his tunic unbuttoned. That was his trademark; it signified that he was an aerial warrior and that he flew fighters. He was, of course, immediately spotted by the opposite sex, young and old, and was instantly admired."

Flight Lieutenant Helen Gardiner, No Forty-third Squadron, RAF: "*Top Gun* came out before I actually joined the Air Force. It was out when I was applying to join the University Air Squadron, and I think it was the big, glamorous 'look what I can do, this is great, and we're all wonderful heroes' and everything is happening at twice the speed . . . I wouldn't say the job is mundane . . . it's not at all, but the movie is exaggerated. Some of the flying sequences are great to watch, but they're not realistic as far as what happens day to day on the squadron . . . the actual stuff that goes with it . . . all the big talk and everything. The Americans themselves might find some of it a little more akin to what they do. But as far as the RAF . . . we operate on a completely different level to what *Top Gun* is showing you. It's something that people watch and they know all the lines to, and it's good fun to throw 'em around every now and again. It's good fun to watch. I don't think there is anybody on the squadron who hasn't seen it, or anybody who would object and say, 'Oh, I'm not watching it; it's rubbish.' It's more of a laugh. Pilots like watching airplanes flying on screen and it always looks brilliant, but I don't think the way they interact with each other is anything quite like what goes on on the squadron."

Major Don Gentile: "Looking back now from my vantage point after some hundreds of scraps with the Germans—of bouncing them and being bounced, and of the bangs and prangs and clobberings, and of being clobbered—I would say now that in those ancient days of 1942 and 1943, the confidence I had in my ability to kill the Nazis and to keep them from killing our men was misplaced. I know how much remained for me to learn before I could handle myself in the rough, fast, big-time company they have operating over Europe. But, in those days I didn't even know how little I knew. After I had a few fights under my belt and made a few scores I became again what I had been before the war—a kid full of beans, who, when he sits in an airplane, feels there is nothing in the world that can master him. Fortunately for me, our side of the war was up against a situation in those years that prevented me from acting on my belief in myself. Otherwise, I probably would have had my beans cooked in some gasoline fire long before I learned how much there is to know besides flying about this business of fighting."

Left: Colonel Francis Gabreski, a famous Thunderbolt ace of the Fifty-sixth Fighter Group in the Second World War; above: Bomber crewmen after returning from a mission.

WARHORSE

Some of the output of the North American Aviation plant at Inglewood, California, in 1943. The bomber in the foreground is a B-25 Mitchell.

The American daylight precision bombing offensive against targets in German-occupied Europe began in the fall of 1942. British Prime Minister Winston Churchill liked the phrase "bombing round the clock" and applied it to the combined bombing offensive of the RAF by night and the

Americans by day, By early spring 1944, several USAAF heavy bomb groups were in place and operating their B-17s and B-24s from bases in the English midlands and East Anglia. These U.S. bases in the English countryside were named after villages they adjoined. They had names like Kimbolton, Eye, Molesworth, Seething, Deenethorpe, and Rattlesden. At a former girls' school in High Wycombe, Bucks., the planners of the American Eighth Air Force developed the missions bomb groups and supporting fighter groups would fly. The requirements for the raids were sent to the bomber and fighter groups by teleprinter the day before the scheduled raid. The groups then followed the teleprinted field order; implementing the bomb, fuel, and ammunition loading, the crew briefings (weather, routes, and timings, anticipated opposition, etc); and then the mission was flown. The takeoff

A pair of P-51D Mustangs escorting a B-17G bomber, three magnificently restored warbirds.

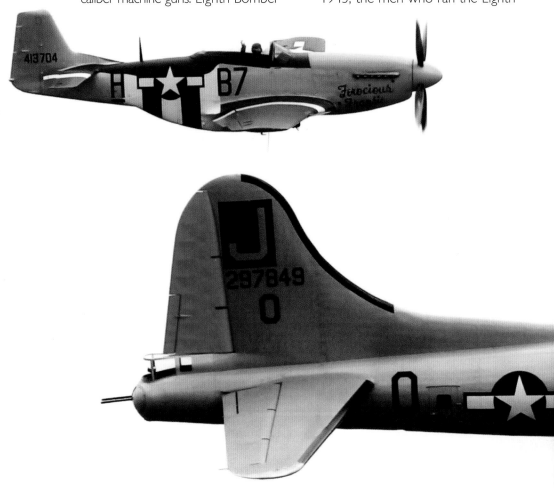

was usually predawn. The extremely time-consuming aircraft assembly into large formations ultimately resulted in a massive bomber stream which then turned on a heading for the target in Europe. Each heavy bomber was armed with as many as thirteen fifty-caliber machine guns. Eighth Bomber Command believed that its B-17s and B-24s, when flown in designed "box formations" within the stream, were capable of defending themselves with cones of gunfire concentrated against the enemy interceptors. That was not the case, however, and, by late 1943, the men who ran the Eighth

had accepted that reality. U.S. bomber losses were unsustainably high and the American bombing campaign against Germany would have to be suspended until a change could be made in their operational method. That change would be equipping the fighter groups of the Eighth with the new Mustang, an aircraft capable of escorting the big bombers all the way to the farthest German targets and back to the bases in England in relative safety and with minimal losses to the bombers and the fighters.

One of the early missions in which the marvelous Mustangs of the Fourth Fighter Group shepherded the bombers, in March 1944, was led in the air by Lt Col James Clark. The target of the day was Berlin, and it was the third trip to the "Big B" for Captain Nicholas "Cowboy" Megura of the Debden-based Fourth. Magura made no bones about his combat attitude. He had

come with the group to shoot down Germans and made sure that everyone in the Fourth knew it. He was among the group's most violent pilots in combat. While seen to be one of the Fourth's more disorderly and boisterous members, he had, in fact, downed two enemy aircraft on each of his two previous outings to Berlin in addition to the destruction of several aircraft on the ground in Germany and a few trains as well. He was looking forward to adding to his score on this day.

A bomber formation ahead called for help and Clark led the pilots of the Fourth racing in a climb to their aid. Just as the his Mustangs reached the threatened bombers, Clark's planes were bounced by five Me-109s from out of the sun. In the next seconds both he and Megura managed to destroy a German fighter. Cowboy was fired on by another enemy airman but was able to shake him off.

He then noticed that a number of enemy fighters were attacking a straggling bomber about a mile away. He soon arrived and began shooting at one of the attacking 109s and was elated to see his tracers find their mark on the engine of the enemy plane. As Megura watched, smoke poured from the enemy plane as the German pilot threw open his canopy and stood up in preparation to bail out—but then the pilot hesitated, possibly considering whether he might still be able land his burning fighter, or if the American pilot might now break off the chase, or even if the American might try to machine-gun him in his parachute. Megura contributed to the German pilot's decision by sending one more short burst of fire in his direction. A second later the German stepped from his cockpit and fell a few hundred feet before his parachute streamed open and jerked him upright.

A restored Mustang on final approach into Duxford airfield in Cambridgeshire.

Up close with this fine restoration of a
P-51D.

Megura was now quite low and near an airfield outside Berlin. He saw some Me 109s circling in the landing pattern and he began following one of them. The German didn't appear to notice the American plane, nor had any of the other German fighter pilots, so Megura positioned himself behind one of the 109s which had its flaps and landing gear down. Before he could fire, however, German fighters roared across the airfield towards him, having recognized the Mustang's profile. The American gave his plane full throttle and was soon able to outdistance them and headed back at low level over the German capital. He soon spotted and shot up a train that happened to be going his way.

He was crossing a range of low hills west of the city when he encountered six more enemy aircraft, which he evaded while weaving through a few valleys. He then gained altitude

and headed on a course for his base at Debden. On the way he came across a lone Junkers Ju-88 known as a *Schnellbomber*. He chased the enemy plane down to roof-top level in an industrial area they were crossing. He fired on the plane but he had little ammunition left and only one working machine gun. His remaining rounds were soon gone so he pulled alongside the slightly damaged German aircraft. In frustration, Cowboy Megura thumbed his nose and yelled something rude at the enemy pilot. Later, he was awarded the Distinguished Service Cross for his actions on that Berlin trip.

A superb example of what many consider the best fighter plane of the Second World War, the North American Mustang.

Painted to resemble *Nookie Bookie*, the P-51
of Major Leonard "Kit" Carson.

The four highest-scoring aces of the
357th Fighter Group in World War II,
left to right: Richard Peterson, Leonard
Carson, John England, and Clarence
Anderson.

Another fine representation of a Fourth Fighter Group P-51, *Darlin' Ann*, about to touch down at the Duxford airfield.

The author is grateful to the following people whose enthusiastic assistance has contributed greatly to the development and preparation of this book. I am particularly indebted to Margaret Mayhew Kaplan for her patience, guidance, consideration, and especially her wise counsel in the course of the work. My thanks to Monique Agazarian, Paddy Barthropp, Malcolm Bates, Diana Barnato-Walker, Mike Benarchik, Nick Berryman, Robert Best, Tony Bianci, Len Biggs, Harold Bird-Wilson, Quentin Bland, Keith Braybrook, Stephen Brooks, Harley Brown, Kazimierz Budzik, John Burgess, Richard Bye, Richard and Pat Collier, Jack Currie, Alan Deere, Bob Doe, Neville Duke, Gary Eastman, David Fairbairn, Gilly Fielder, Lou Christian, Wilson Fleming, Sir Christopher Foxley-Norris, Roger Freeman, Ella Freire, Royal Frey, Dave Glaser, James Goodson, James Gray, Beryl Green, Stephen Grey, Jonathan Grimwood, Roger Hall, R. C. Harris Jr., George Hazel, Jack Heath, Bill Hess, Robin Higham, Dave Hill, Robert Hofton, Eric Holloway, Tony Iacono, Jack Ilfrey, Lynn Johnson, Neal Kaplan, Brian Kingcome, Walter Konantz, Edith Kup, Jimmy Kyle, Chrystabel Leighton-Porter, Robert Loomis, Walker M. Mahurin, Eric Marsden, Mike Mathews, Carroll McColpin, Bert McDowell, Tilly McMaster, Len Morgan, John Newth, Leo Nomis, Michael O'Leary, Merle Olmsted, W. Bruce PICOverstreet, Charles Neville Overton, Geoffrey Page, Jeffrey Quill, Gordon and Winston Ramsey, Jack Raphael, Alan Reeves, Mark Ritchie, Denis Robinson, Arthur Roscoe, Andy Saunders, Eudora Seyfer, Ann and Richard Stamp, Ulrich Steinhilper, Bert Stiles, Robert Strobell, The Yanks Air Museum, Chino, Peter Townsend, California, Anne and Dickey Turley-George, George Unwin, Mary and Keith Vanstone, Chris von Glahn, David Wade, Jock Wells, Tim Wells, Ray Wild, Frank Wootton, and Hub Zemke.

PICTURE CREDITS

Images by the author are credited PK; images provided by the United States National Archives are credited NARA; images from the collection of the author are credited AC. P3: PK, P4: Cuthbert Orde, P6: AC, P9: PK, P10: AC, P12: AC, PP14-15: Allan Burney, PP16-17: NARA, P18 top left: PK, center: U.S. Air Force, bottom: PK, P19 top: U.S. Air Force, P21: courtesy Robert Cooper, P22: courtesy Quentin Bland, P23: PK, P25: AC, PP26-27: PK, P28 top: AC, bottom: PK, P29: Cuthbert Orde, PP30-31: Allan Burney, PP32-33: Bundesarchiv, PP34-35: PK, P36: AC, P37: PK, PP38-39: Allan Burney, P40: AC, PP42-43: Michael O'Leary, P44 top: courtesy Jack Ilfrey, bottom: AC, P45: courtesy Jack Ilfrey, PP46-47: AC, P48: Simon Thomas, P49: John Myers, P51: AC, PP52-53: Mike Durning, PP54-55: G. Phelps, PP56-57: AC, P59: AC, PP60-61: AC, PP62-63: AC, P64: AC, P65: PK, P66 top: AC, bottom: PK, P67: AC,. P68: Charles E. Brown, P69: U.S. Air Force, PP70-71: courtesy Jack Currie, P72: Bundesarchiv, P73: Bundesarchiv, P75: Bundesarchiv, P76: AC, P77: PK, P78: AC, P79 both: AC, P80 top: AC, bottom both: AC, PP82-83: AC. PP84-85: Zdenek Ondracek, P86: AC, P89: Frank Wootton, P90 left: PK, right: AC, P91: PK, PP92-93: PK, P94: AC, P95: AC, P96: courtesy Eric Marsden, P97: courtesy Oscar Boesch, P99 top: PK, bottom left: AC, bottom right: courtesy Geoffrey Page, P100: Cuthbert Orde, P103: AC, P105: AC, P107: Allan Burney, P108: PK, P109: AC, P110 both: AC, P111: PK, P112: Bundesarchiv, P114: AC, PP116-117: AC, P118: AC, PP120-121: AC, PP122-123: Bundesarchiv: P124: AC, P125: AC, P126: Gary Chambers, P128: AC, P129: AC, PP130-131: DeGolyer Library, P132 both: AC, P133: AC, P134: AC, P135: AC, P136: DeGolyer Library, PP138-139: DeGolyer Library, PP140-141: PK, P142: DeGolyer Library, P143: AC, P144: courtesy Ray Wild, P146 top: AC, bottom: AC, P147: PK, P148: PK, P149 all: AC, P150 top left: AC, center: PK, Bottom: U.S. Air Force, P151: PK, P153: AC, P154-155 all: PK, P155 bottom right: AC, P156: PK, P159: AC, P161: AC, PP162-163: NARA, P164: Cuthbert Orde, P166: AC, P167: AC, P169: PK, PP170-171: AC, P172: AC, P173: AC, P174 both: AC, P175: AC, PP176-177: Vickers, P178: PK, P179: courtesy Merle Olmsted, P180: John Myers, P181: PK, P182: PK, P183: Toni Frissell, PP184-185: NARA, P186: PK, P187: NARA, P188: AC, P189: courtesy Merle Olmsted, P191: PK, PP192-193: AC, P196 all: AC, P197: AC, P198: DeGolyer Library, P199: AC, PP200-201: AC, P202: AC, P203: AC, P204: DeGolyer Library, bottom: AC, P205 all: AC, P206: AC, P207: AC, P208 top, AC, bottom: AC, P209: PK, PP210-211: AC, P212: AC, P214: AC, P216: AC, P217: AC, PP218-219: PK, PP220-221: San Diego Aerospace Museum, PP222-223: Zdenek Ondracek, PP224-225: Michael Brazier, PP226-227: Mike Durning, PP228-229: GaryChambers, PP230-231: Zdenek Ondracek, PP232-233: courtesy Merle Olmsted, PP234-235: Simon Thomas. P237: Toni Frissell.

BIBLIOGRAPHY

Bekker, Cajus, *The Luftwaffe War Diaries*, Doubleday & Co., 1968.
Bishop, Edward, *The Battle of Britain*, Allen and Unwin, 1960.
Bishop, Edward, *The Guinea Pig Club*, New English Library, 1963.
Blake, *Readiness At Dawn*, Victor Gollancz Ltd., 1941.
Brickhill, Paul, *Reach For The Sky*,

Collins, 1954.

Collier, Richard, *Eagle Day*, Pan Books, 1968.

Crook, D. M., *Spitfire Pilot*, Faber & Faber

Deere, Alan, *Nine Lives*, Coronet Books, 1959.

Deighton, Len, *Fighter*, Ballantine Books, 1977.

Dundas, Hugh, *Flying Start*, St Martin's Press, 1989.

Forrester, Larry, *Fly For Your Life*, Bantam Books, 1977.

Foxley-Norris, Sir Christopher, *A Lighter Shade of Blue*, Ian Allen, 1978.

Franks, Norman, *Sky Tiger*, Crecy,1980.

Freeman, Roger, *Mighty Eighth War Diary*, Jane's, 1981.

Galland, Adolf, *The First and the Last*, Ballantine Books, 1954.

Gallico, Paul, *The Hurricane Story*, Four Square Books, 1967.

Glancey, Jonathan, *Spitfire: The Biography*, Atlantic Books, 2006.

Godfrey, John, *The Look of Eagles*, Random House, 1958.

Goodson, James, *Tumult in the Clouds*, St Martin's Press, 1983.

Gurney, Gene, *Five Down and Glory*, Ballantine Books, 1958.

Haining, Peter, *The Spitfire Log*, Souvenir Press, 1985.

Hall, Grover, *1000 Destroyed*, Aero Publishers, Inc., 1978.

Hall, Roger, *Clouds of Fear*, Coronet Books, 1975.

Henshaw, Alex, *Sigh For A Merlin*, Hamlyn, 1979.

Hillary, Richard, *The Last Enemy*, Pan Books, 1942.

Ilfrey, Jack, *Happy Jack's Go-Buggy*, Exposition Press, 1979.

Johnson, J. E., *Wing Leader*, Chatto & Windus, 1956.

Kaplan, Philip, *Fighter Pilot*, Aurum Press, 1999.

Kaplan, Philip and Collier, Richard, *The Few*, Blandford Press, 1989.

Kaplan, Philip and Smith, Rex Alan, *One Last Look*, Abbeville Press, 1983.

Kingcome, Brian, *A Willingness to Die*, Tempus, 1999.

Loomis, Robert D., *Great American Fighter Pilots of World War II*, Random House, 1961.

Lyall, Gavin, *The War in the Air*, Ballantine Books, 1968.

Mason, F. K., *Battle Over Britain*, McWhirter Twins, 1969.

Mitchell, Gordon, *Schooldays to Spitfire*, Tempus, 1986.

Ogley, Bob, *Biggin on the Bump*, Froglets Publications, 1990.

Orde, Cuthbert, *Pilots of Fighter Command*, George G. Harrap, 1942.

Page, Geoffrey, *Tale of a Guinea Pig*, Pelham Books Ltd., 1981.

Peaslee, Budd J., *Heritage of Valor*, J. B. Lippincott Company, 1964.

Quill, Jeffrey, *Birth of a Legend The Spitfire*, Quiller Press, 1986.

Speer, Frank, *Wingman*, Carlton, 1993.

Tidy, Douglas, *I Fear No Man*, Macdonald and Co., 1972.

Townsend, Peter, *Duel of Eagles*, Simon & Schuster, 1970.

INDEX